CONTENTS

DO IT YOURSELF: ROCK GUITAR

About the Cloud

DiY is an interactive multimedia experience—with video and audio demonstrations available for every lesson, example, and song in the book. You can stream or download corresponding media to your computer or mobile device wherever you see the download icon. Simply follow along in the book, and you will have everything you need.

To access the accompanying media, go to **alfred.com/redeem** and enter the code found on the inside front cover of this book.

Alfred Music
P.O. Box 10003
Van Nuys, CA 91410-0003
alfred.com

ISBN-10: 1-4706-1138-4 (Book & Media)
ISBN-13: 978-1-4706-1138-5 (Book & Media)

Cover photo courtesy of Gibson USA

Gears: © iStockphoto / aleksandarvelasevic • Blueprint: © iStockphoto / Branislav

Alfred Cares. Contents printed on environmentally responsible paper.

THE PARTS OF THE GUITAR

DO IT YOURSELF: ROCK GUITAR

Acoustic

Headstock
Tuning Pegs
Nut
Strings
Neck, Fretboard, Fingerboard (includes all frets)
Fret Wire
Position Marker
Soundhole
Waist
Bridge
Body

Electric

Headstock
Tuning Pegs
Nut
Fret Wire
Neck, Fretboard, Fingerboard (includes all frets)
Strings
Strap Peg
Position Marker
Cutaway
Tremolo (Whammy) Bar
Waist
Pickups
Pickup Selector Switch
Bridge
Volume
Tone Controls
Tailpiece
Output Jack
Body
Strap Peg

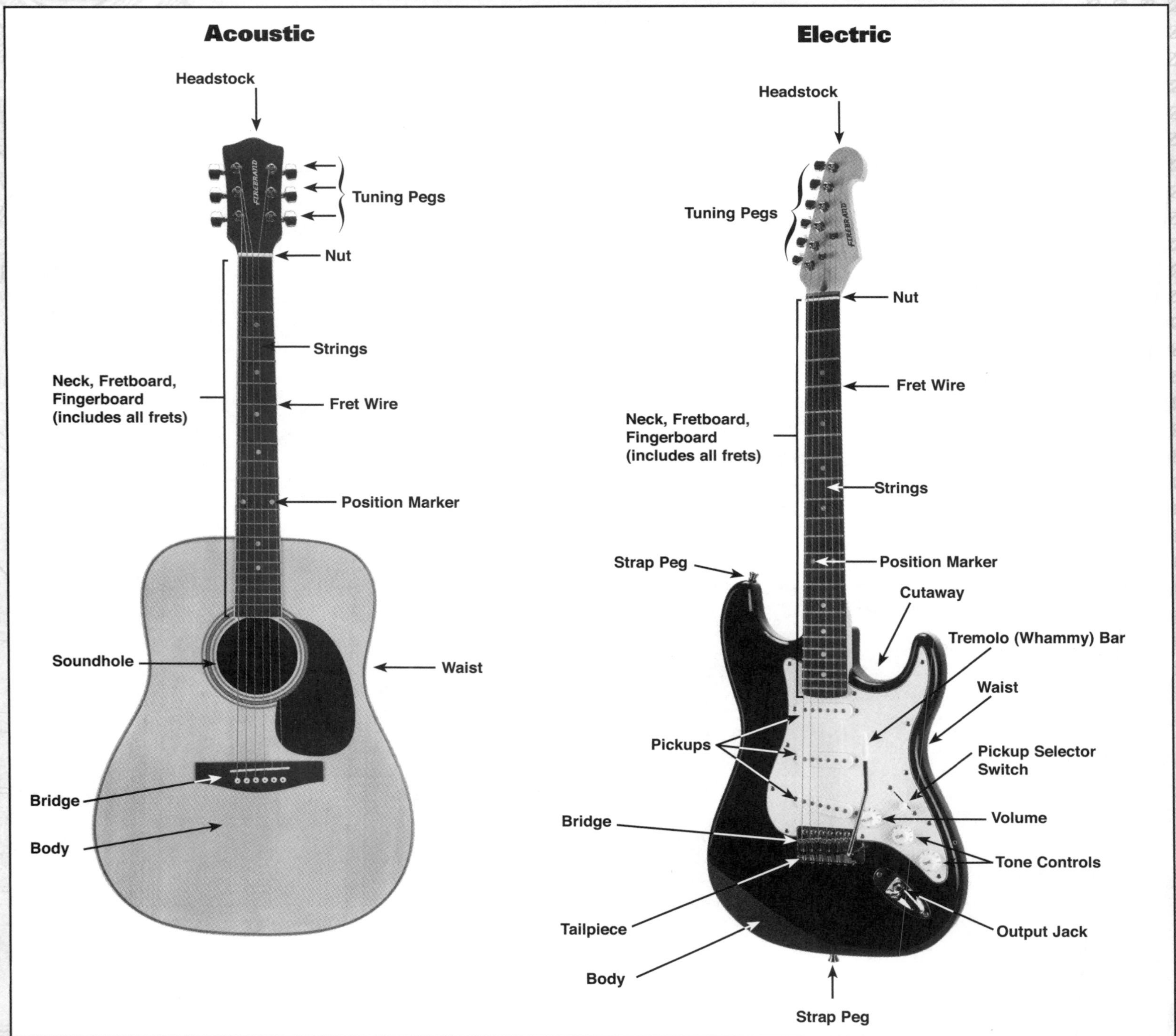

WHICH GUITAR IS BEST FOR ME?

DO IT YOURSELF: ROCK GUITAR

Which guitar is the "right" guitar for you? It's all a matter of taste, what kind of music you want to play, and what you want to sound like. Some beginners say a nylon-string guitar is easier on their fingers, but eventually you're going to get calluses and become accustomed to any guitar you practice on. The most important consideration is probably the size: if you have small hands, you will find a smaller guitar easier to play. Also, a guitar with a very big, fat body will be hard for a small person to manage. It's just common sense. If you want to rock out, it's perfectly fine to start learning on an electric guitar—there are no rules about which guitar to get first. Get one that you will want to pick up and play every day!

HOW TO HOLD YOUR GUITAR

DO IT YOURSELF: ROCK GUITAR

Hold your guitar in a position that is most comfortable for you. Some positions are shown below. When playing, keep your left wrist away from the fingerboard. This will allow your fingers to be in a better position to finger the chords. Press your fingers firmly, but make sure they do not touch the neighboring strings.

Tilt the neck slightly up. Don't twist the body of the guitar to see the strings better.

Standing with strap.

Sitting.

Sitting with legs crossed.

THE AMPLIFIER

DO IT YOURSELF: ROCK GUITAR

If you are playing an electric guitar, you will need to use an *amplifier*. The amplifier (or amp) makes the sound of a guitar louder and allows you to add effects, like distortion, to your sound. All amps are different, but here are a few features you will find on virtually every amp.

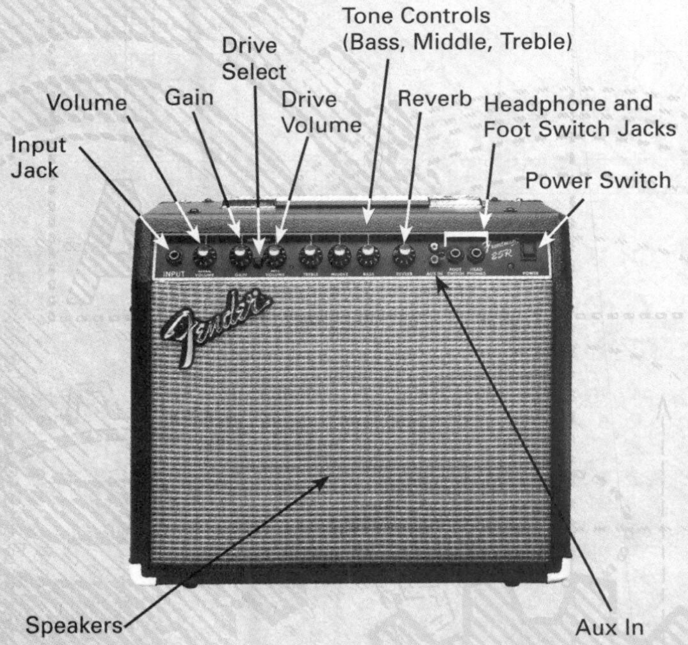

Aux In: RCA input jacks for use with a portable CD or tape player, drum machine, etc.

Input Jacks: This is where you plug in your guitar with a ¼" plug.

Drive Select: Activates the Drive channel.

Drive Volume: Controls the loudness of the Drive channel.

Headphone and Foot Switch Jacks: Plug in your optional foot switch for changing channels, or your mono or stereo headphones.

Gain: This control, sometimes called "drive," will adjust the amount of distortion added to your sound.

Power Switch: This switch turns the unit ON and OFF.

Reverb: Reverb adds an echo sound to your playing. Not all amps have this feature.

Speakers: The sound comes directly out of the amp through the speakers. Be careful not to touch the speakers because they are easily damaged.

Tone Controls: You can adjust the high (treble), middle, and low (bass) sounds of your guitar. Adjust these controls to find a sound you like.

Volume: The higher the number, the louder the sound. Be aware of who is around you before turning up the volume.

THE RIGHT HAND

Strumming with a Pick

Hold the pick between your thumb and index finger. Grip it firmly, but don't squeeze too hard.

Strum from the 6th string (the thickest, lowest-sounding string) to the 1st string (the thinnest, highest-sounding string).

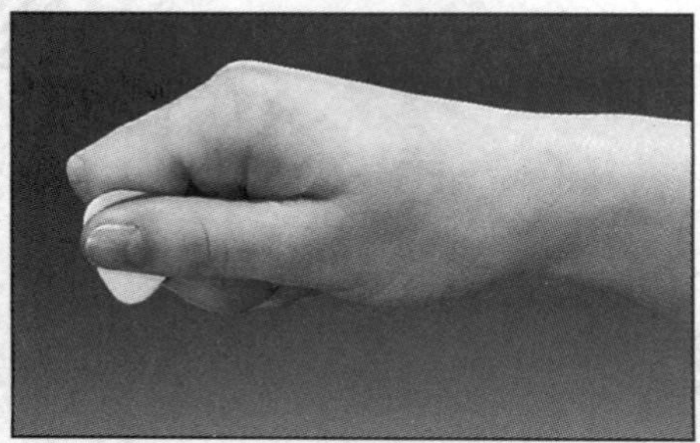

Correct way to hold a pick.

Important: Strum by mostly moving your wrist, not just your arm. Use as little motion as possible. Start as close to the thickest string as you can, and never let your hand move past the edge of the guitar.

Start near the thickest string.

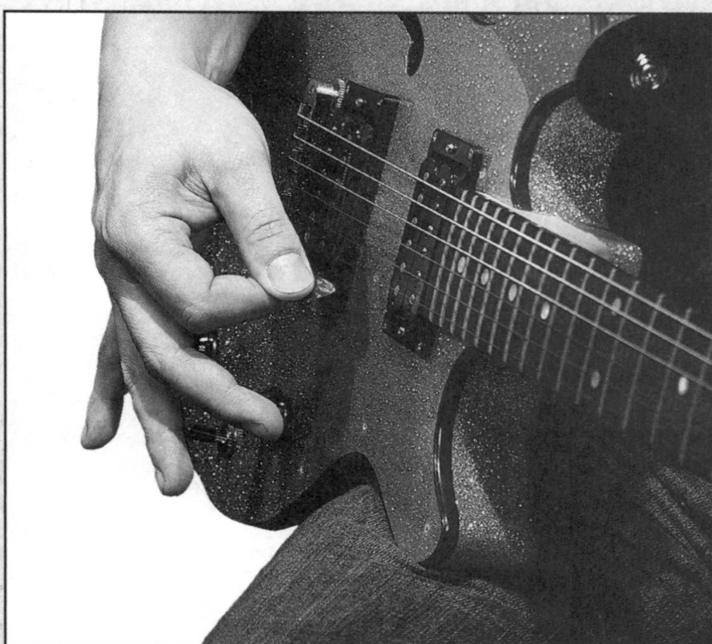

Move mostly your wrist, not just your arm. Finish near the thinnest string.

THE LEFT HAND

Proper Left-Hand Position

Learning to use your left-hand fingers starts with a good hand position. Place your hand so your thumb rests comfortably in the middle of the back of the neck. Position your fingers on the strings as if you are gently squeezing a ball between them and your thumb. Keep your elbow in and your fingers curved.

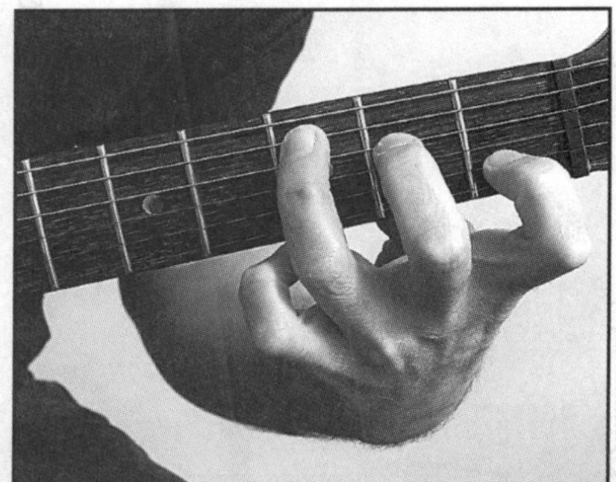

Keep your elbow in and fingers curved. Arch your wrist slightly so your fingertips can more easily come down on top of the strings.

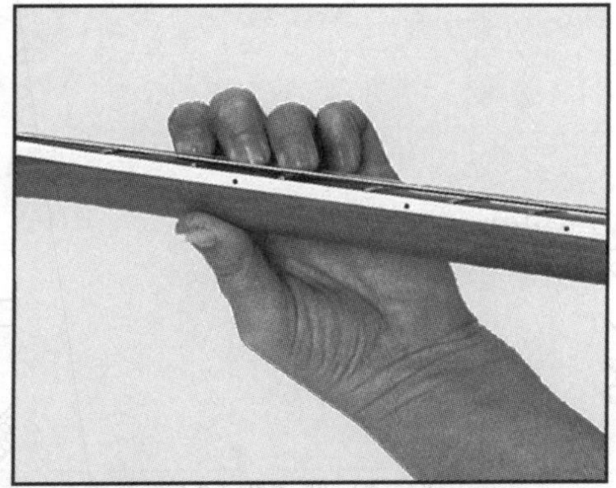

Position fingers as if you are gently squeezing a ball between your fingertips and thumb. Place the thumb behind the fingerboard opposite the 2nd finger.

Placing a Finger on a String

When you press a string with a left-hand finger, make sure you press firmly with the tip of your finger and as close to the fret wire as you can without actually being right on it. Short fingernails are important! This will create a clean, bright tone.

Right!
Finger presses the string down near the fret without actually being on it.

Wrong!
Finger is too far from the fret wire; the tone is "buzzy" and indefinite.

Wrong!
Finger is on top of the fret wire; the tone is muffled and unclear.

TUNING YOUR GUITAR

First, make sure your strings are wound properly around the tuning pegs. They should go from the inside to the outside as illustrated to the right. Some guitars have all six tuning pegs on the same side of the headstock. If this is the case, make sure all six strings are wound the same way, from the inside out.

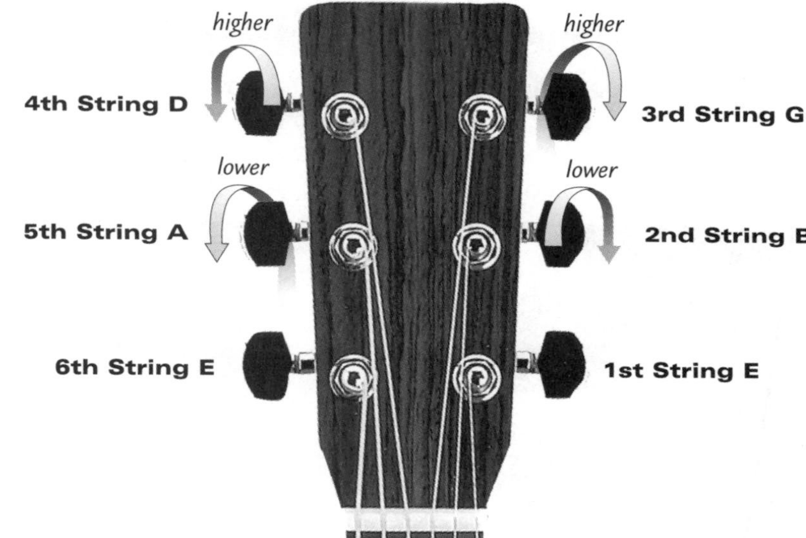

Turning a tuning peg clockwise makes the pitch lower. Turning a tuning peg counterclockwise makes the pitch higher. Be sure not to tune the strings too high because they could break.

Important:

Always remember that the thinnest, highest-sounding string, the one closest to the floor, is the first string. The thickest, lowest-sounding string, the one closest to the ceiling, is the sixth string. When guitarists say "the highest string," they are referring to the highest-sounding string.

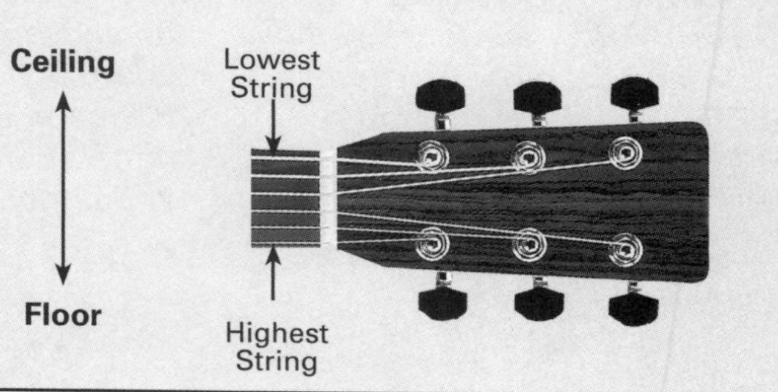

Tuning to the Online Media

When tuning while watching the online media, listen to the directions and match each of your guitar's strings to the corresponding pitches on the online media.

Tuning the Guitar to Itself

When your sixth string is in tune, you can tune the rest of the strings using the guitar alone. First, tune the sixth string to E on the piano:

Then, follow the instructions below to get the guitar in tune.

Press 5th fret of 6th string to get pitch of 5th string (A).

Press 5th fret of 5th string to get pitch of 4th string (D).

Press 5th fret of 4th string to get pitch of 3rd string (G).

Press 4th fret of 3rd string to get pitch of 2nd string (B).

Press 5th fret of 2nd string to get pitch of 1st string (E).

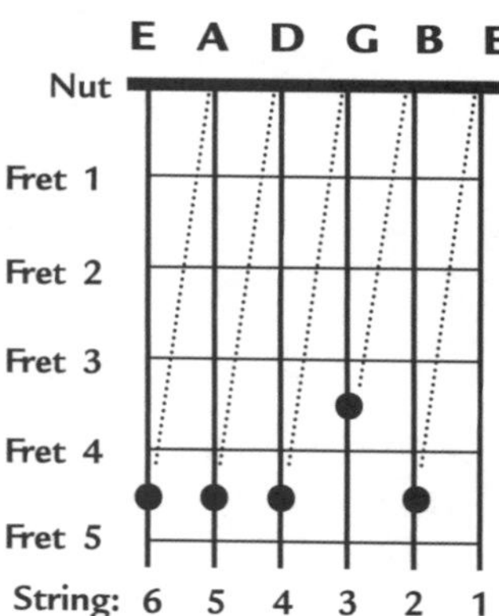

Pitch Pipes and Electronic Tuners

If you don't have a piano available, consider buying an electronic tuner or pitch pipe. There are many types available, and a salesperson at your local music store can help you decide which is best for you.

THE BASICS OF READING MUSIC

Musical sounds are indicated by symbols called *notes.* Their time value is determined by their color (white or black) and by stems or flags attached to the note.

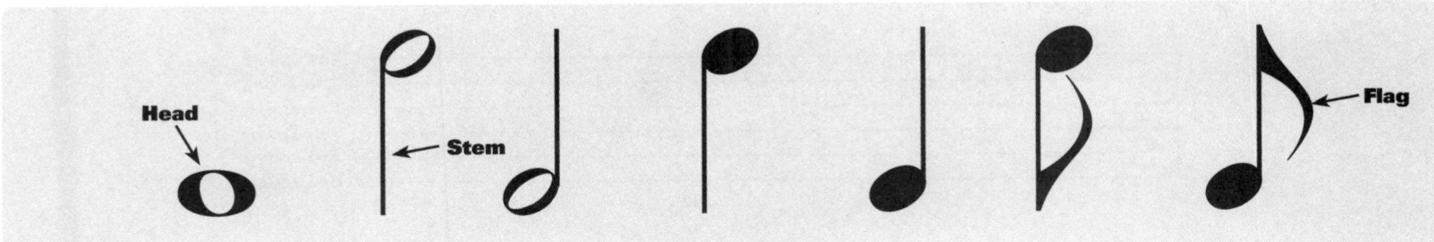

The Staff

The notes are named after the first seven letters of the alphabet (A–G), which are repeated to embrace the entire range of musical sound. The name and pitch of a note are determined by the note's position on the *staff,* which is made up of five horizontal lines and four spaces between.

5th LINE
4th SPACE
4th LINE
3rd SPACE
3rd LINE
2nd SPACE
2nd LINE
1st SPACE
1st LINE

The Treble Clef

During the evolution of musical notation, the staff had from 2 to 20 lines, and symbols were invented to locate certain lines and the pitch of the note on that line. These symbols were called *clefs.*

Music for the guitar is written in the *G clef,* or *treble clef.* Originally the Gothic letter G was used on a four-line staff to establish the pitch of G.

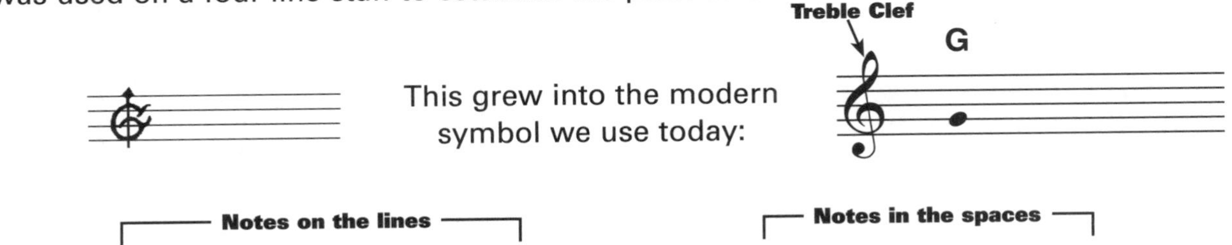

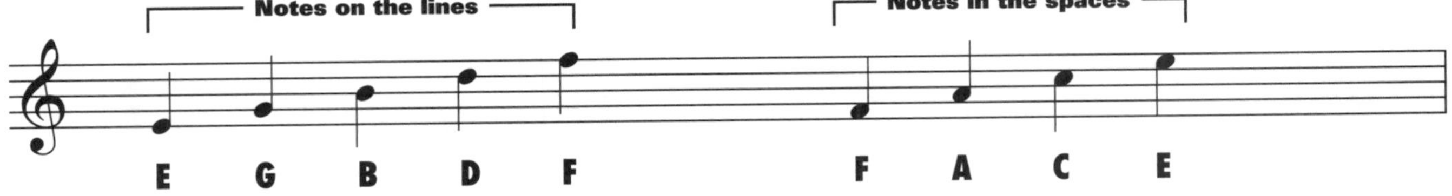

Measures (Bars)

Music is also divided into equal parts called *measures,* or *bars.* One measure is divided from another by a *bar line*:

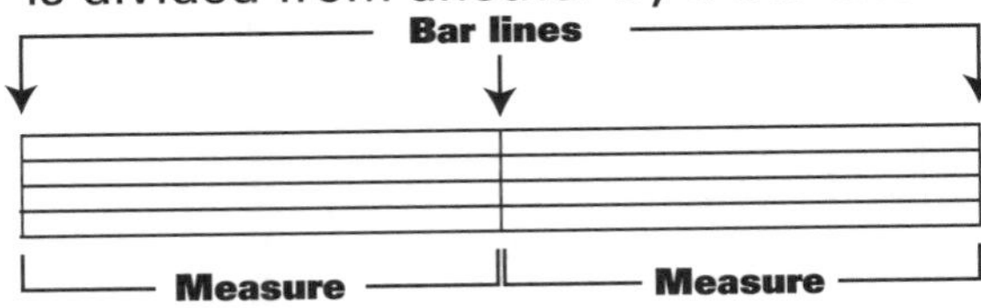

Reading TAB

All the music in this book is written two ways: in standard music notation and in *TAB*. Below each standard music staff you'll find a six-line TAB staff. Each line represents a string of the guitar, with the highest, thinnest string at the top and the lowest, thickest string at the bottom.

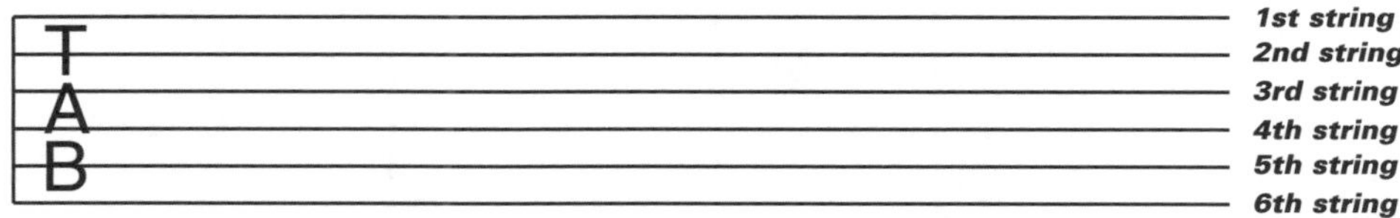

Numbers placed on the TAB lines tell you which fret to play. A zero means to play the string open (not fingered).

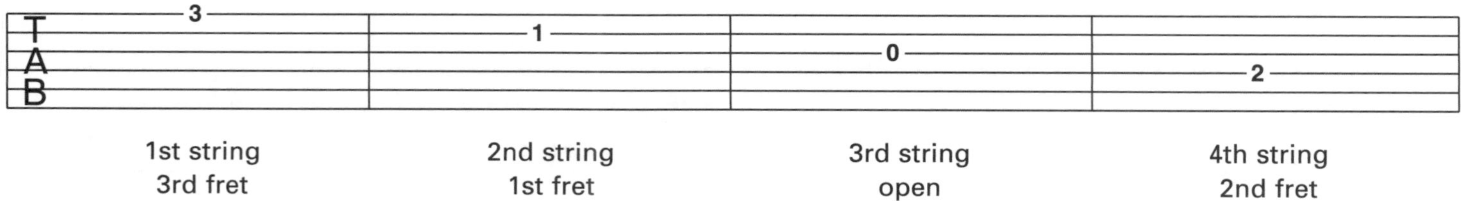

1st string 3rd fret | 2nd string 1st fret | 3rd string open | 4th string 2nd fret

Numbers placed one on top of the other are played at the same time.

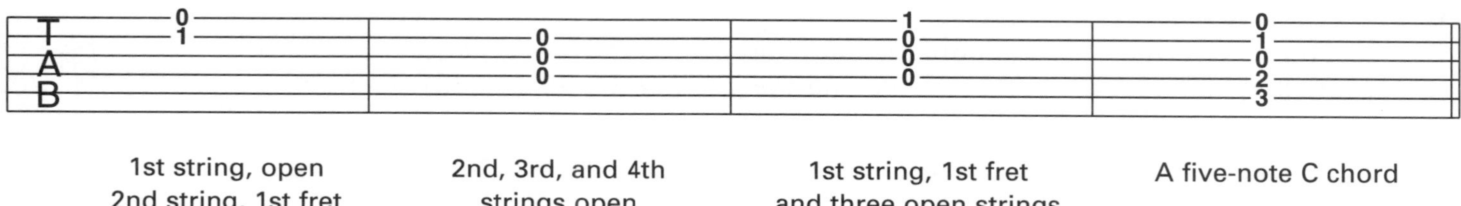

1st string, open 2nd string, 1st fret | 2nd, 3rd, and 4th strings open | 1st string, 1st fret and three open strings | A five-note C chord

By glancing at the TAB, you can immediately tell where to play a note. Although you can't tell exactly what the rhythm is from the TAB, the horizontal spacing of the numbers gives you a strong hint about how long or short the notes are to be played.

Chord Diagrams

Chord diagrams are used to indicate fingering for chords. The example to the right means to place your first finger on the 1st fret, 2nd string, and second finger on the 2nd fret, 4th string. Then strum the first four strings only. The x's on the 5th and 6th strings indicate not to play these.

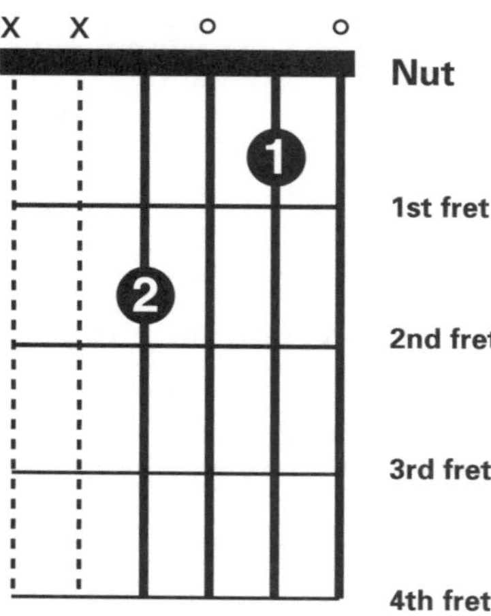

NOTES ON THE SIXTH STRING E

DO IT YOURSELF: ROCK GUITAR

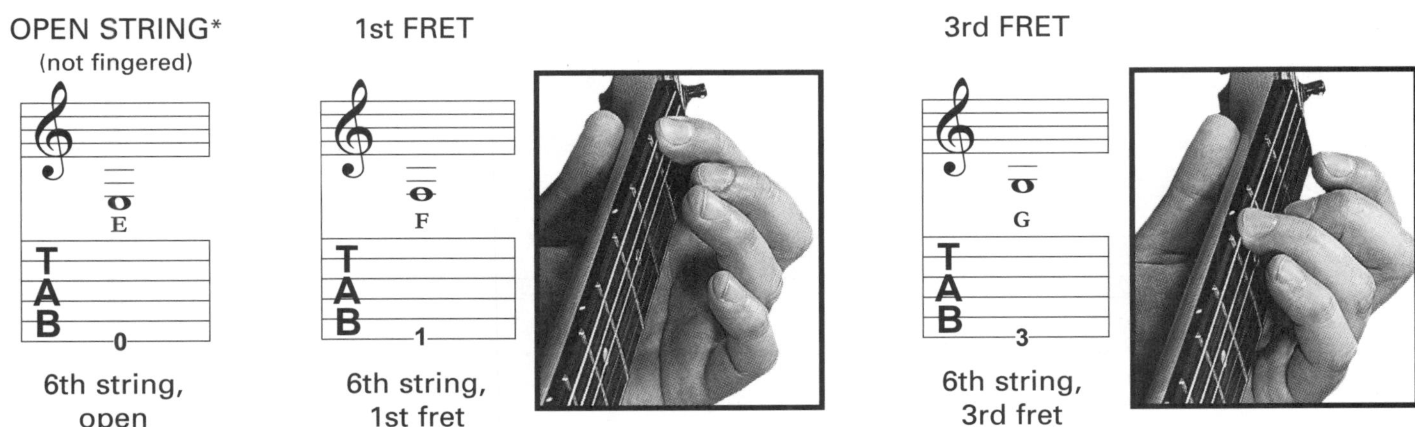

Play the song slowly and evenly. Use only down-strokes, indicated by ⊓. The symbol ○ under or over a note means *open string.* Do not finger.

A FINAL DOUBLE BAR SHOWS THE END OF AN EXAMPLE OR SONG.

SIXTH-STRING RIFF 1

A *riff* is a short, repeated melodic pattern.

SIXTH-STRING RIFF 2

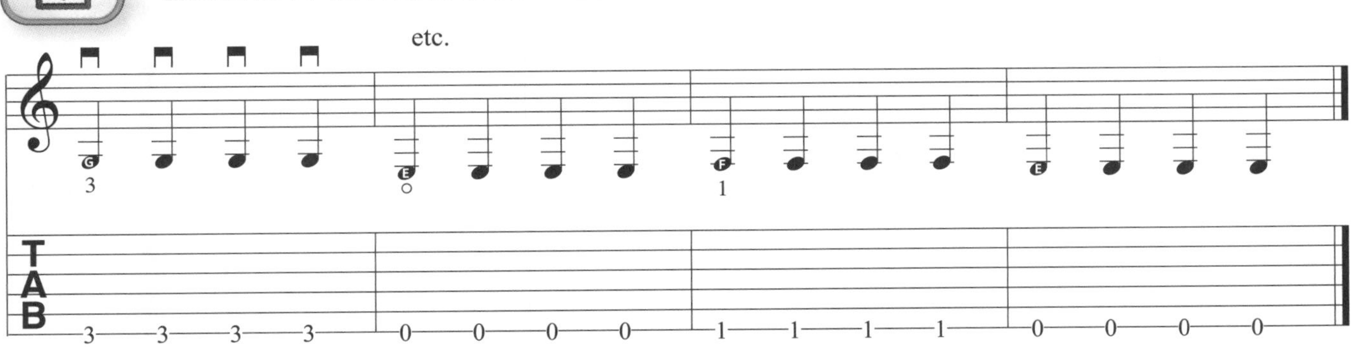

* Though no photo is shown for the open string, the fingers of the left hand should remain slightly above the string, ready to play the correct fret when needed. The thumb should also remain in its proper position.

MORE RIFFS

STILL MORE RIFFS

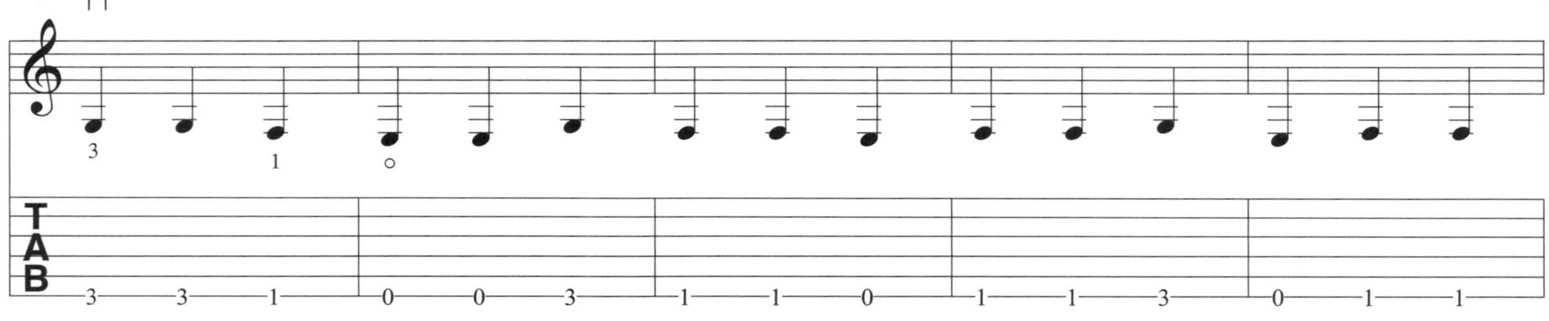

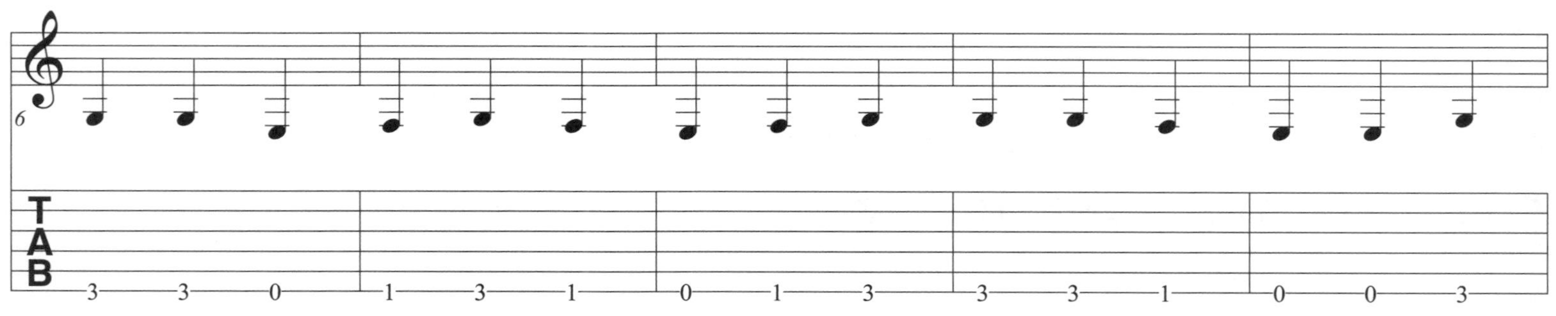

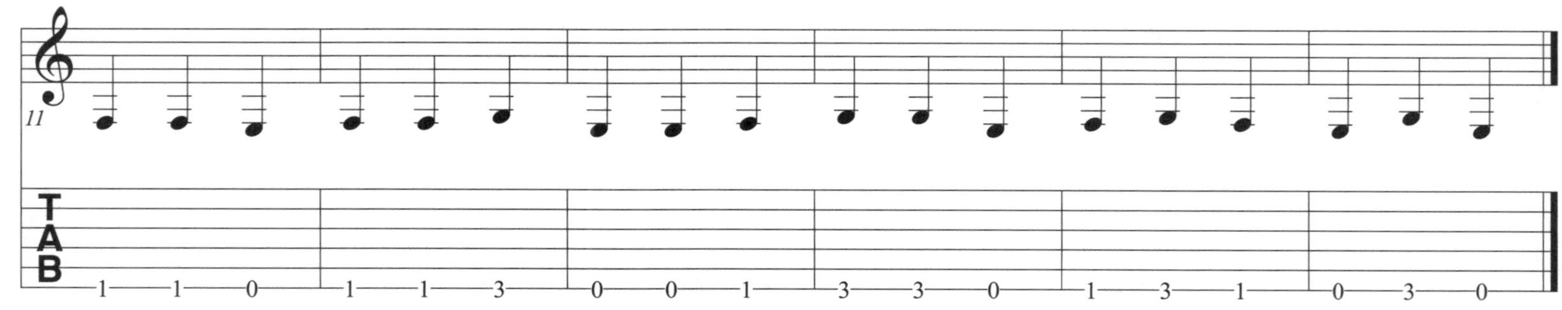

ROCKIN' BASS LINE

TAB:
0 0 0 1 | 3 3 3 1 | 0 0 0 3 | 0 0 0 3

5
0 0 0 1 | 3 3 3 1 | 0 0 0 3 | 0 0 0 1

9
3 3 3 0 | 3 3 1 0 | 1 1 1 3 | 1 1 3 1

13
0 0 0 1 | 3 3 3 1 | 0 0 0 3 | 0 0 0 0

Silent Guitar Calisthenics 1 and 2

This exercise is silent because it is done with the left hand alone. The goal is to go as slowly as possible, keeping one finger down on the string as you add the other, and pressing the string down more firmly than usual. You are working on the muscles that spread the fingers apart, and this will help develop your reach. Use the left side of the tip of your 1st finger and the exact middle of the tip of your 3rd finger. Remember to place the fingers just to the left of the frets.

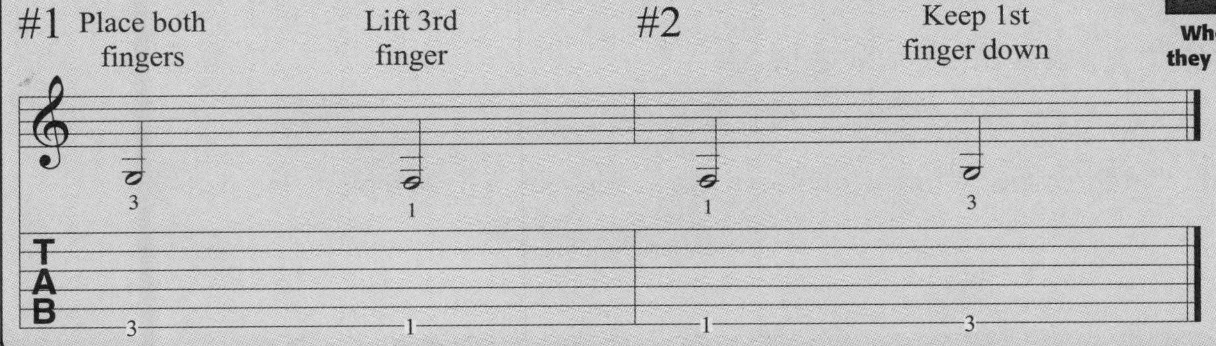

When both fingers are down, they should look similar to this.

SOUND OFF: HOW TO COUNT TIME

Four Kinds of Notes

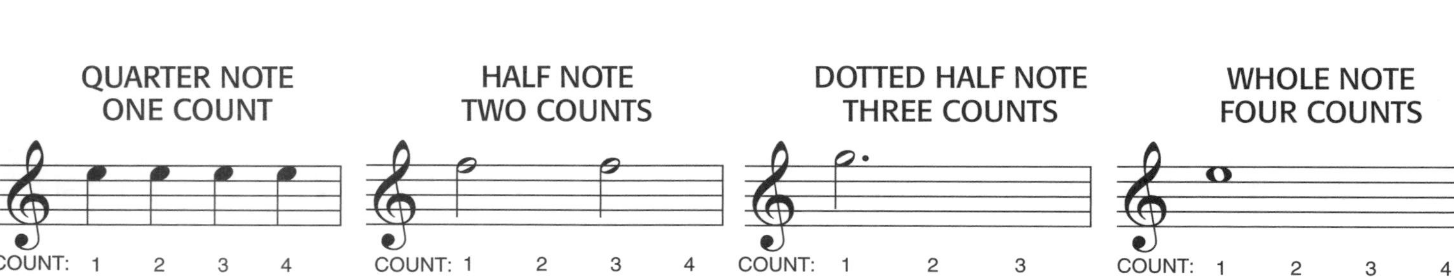

Time Signatures

Each piece of music has numbers at the beginning called a *time signature*. These numbers tell us how to count time.

The TOP NUMBER tells us how many counts are in each measure.
The BOTTOM NUMBER tells us what kind of note gets one count.

FOUR COUNTS TO A MEASURE

A QUARTER NOTE GETS ONE COUNT

THREE COUNTS TO A MEASURE

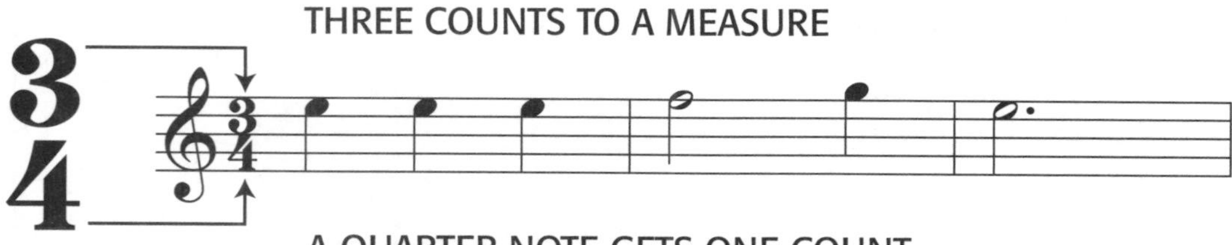

A QUARTER NOTE GETS ONE COUNT

Important: Go back and fill in the missing time signatures of the songs you have already learned.

NOTES ON THE FIFTH STRING A

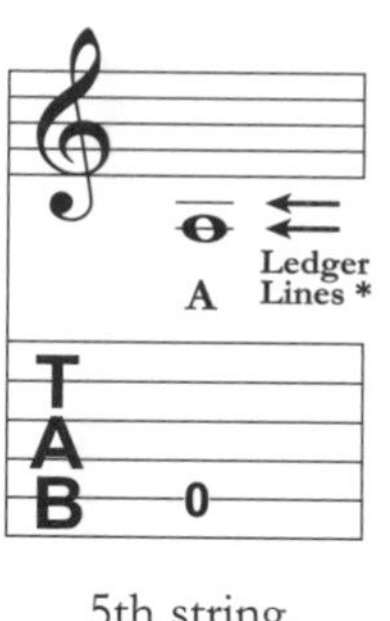

5th string, open

2nd FRET

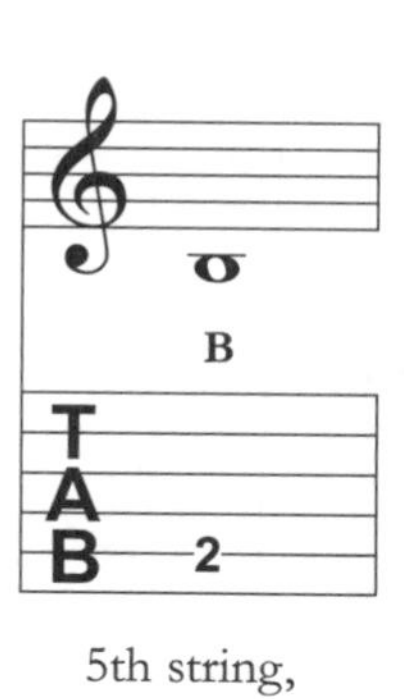

5th string, 2nd fret

3rd FRET

5th string, 3rd fret

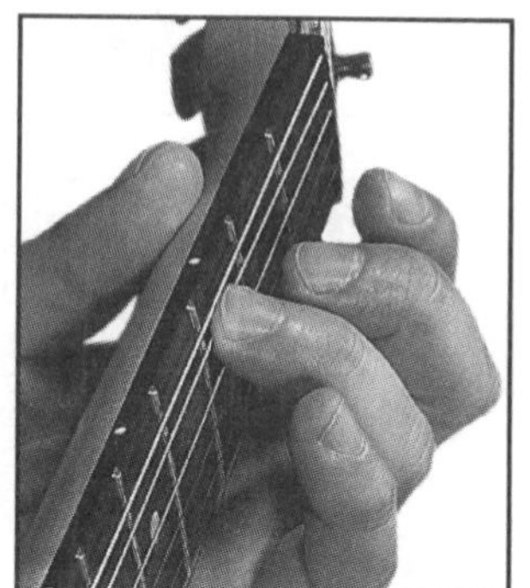

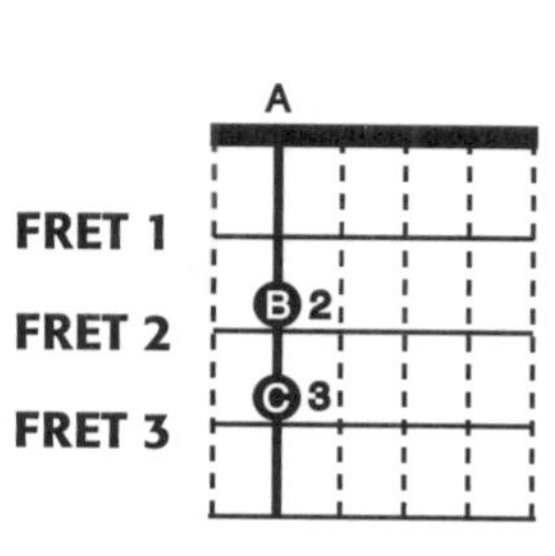

JAMMING ON 5 AND 6

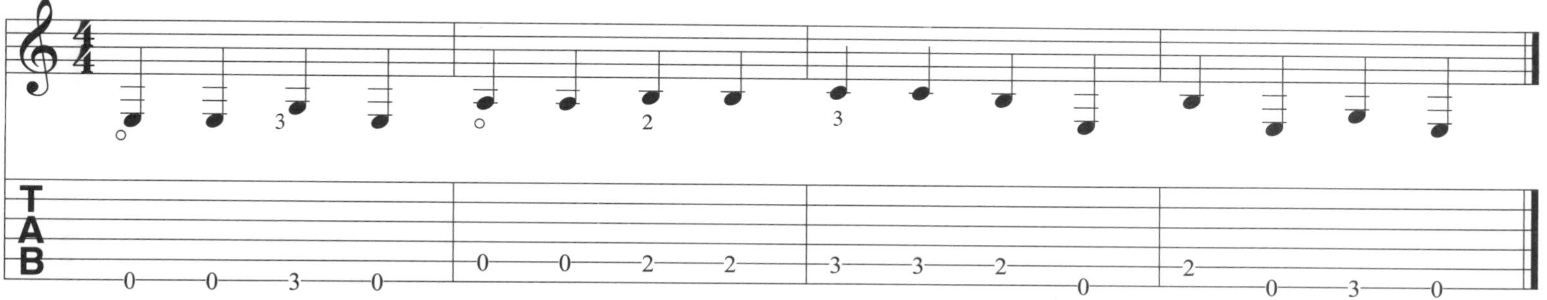

TWO-STRING ROCK

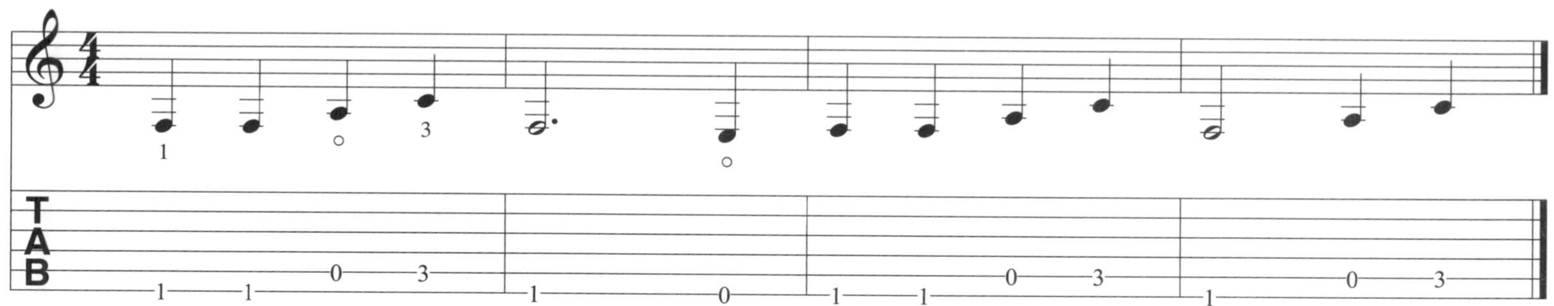

* The short line that extends the staff downwards is called a *ledger line*. You already used them for E, F, and G.

EASY ROCK RIFFS ON THE FIFTH AND SIXTH STRINGS

Repeat Signs

The double dots inside the double bars are *repeat signs*, and they indicate that everything between the double bars must be repeated.

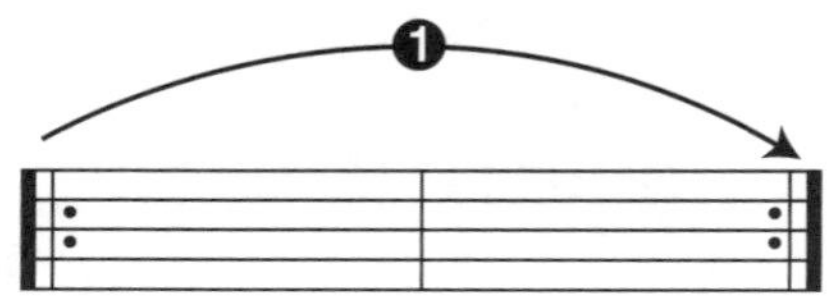

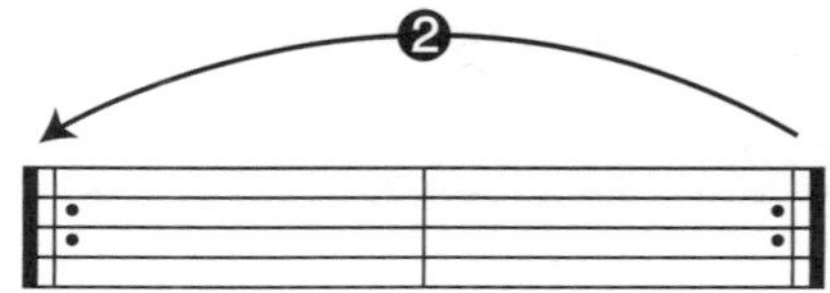

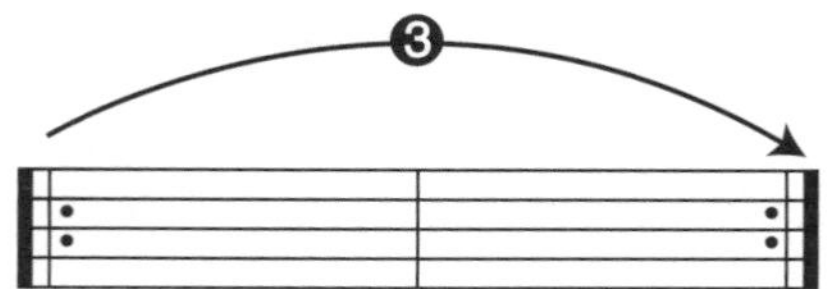

KING LOUIE

The following example is in the style of The Kingsmen's major hit, "Louie Louie."

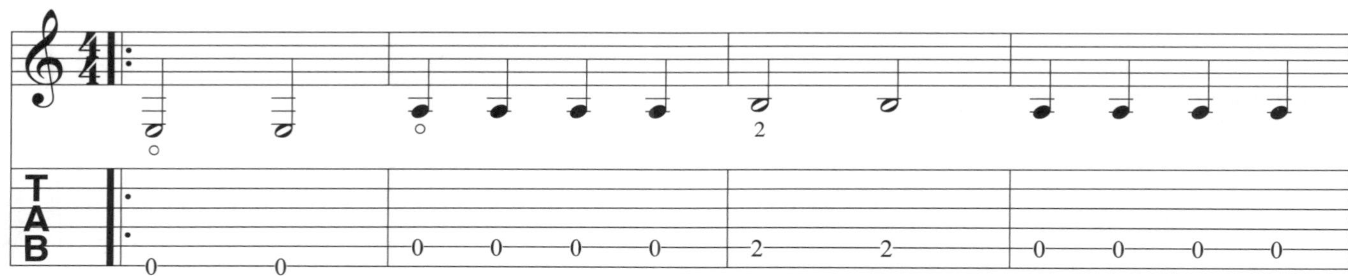

AS I ARRIVE

This one's in the style of the classic Green Day song "When I Come Around."

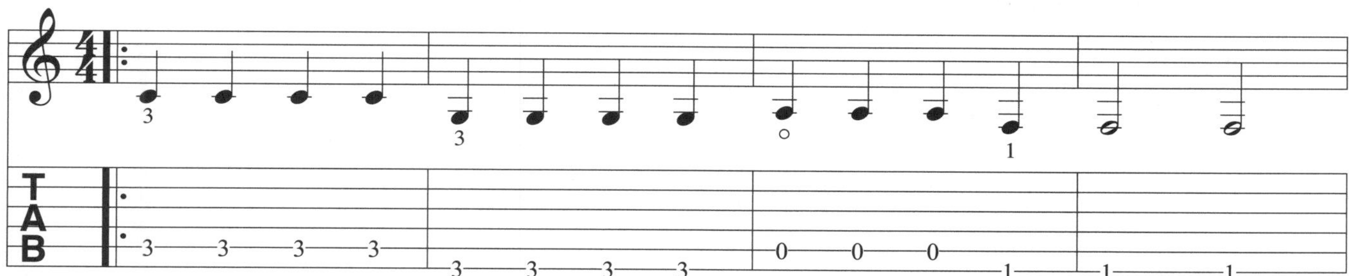

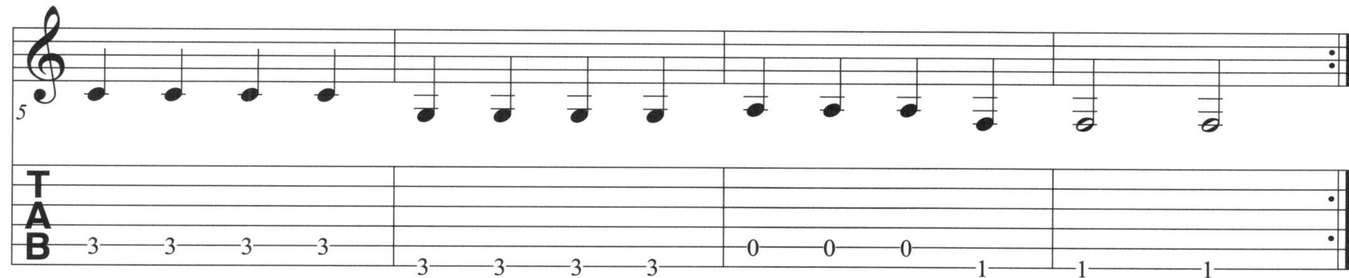

FERROUS GUY

The riff below is in the style of "Iron Man" by Black Sabbath.

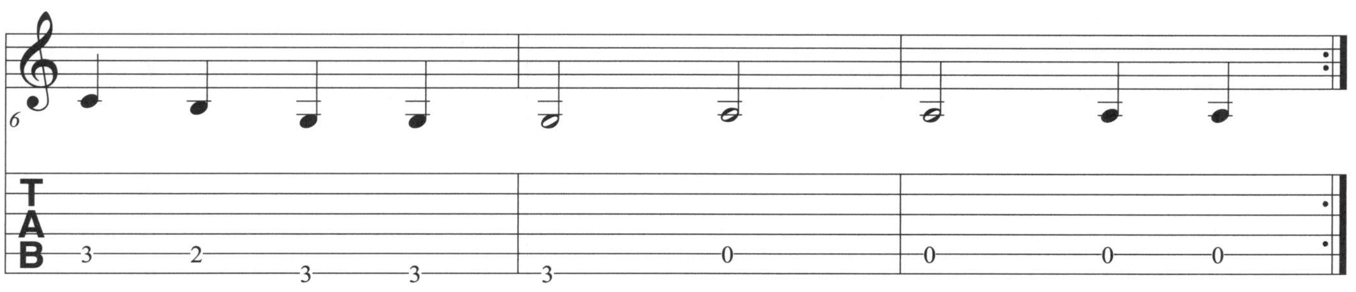

THEY CAN ROCK

This is in the style of Queen's huge hit "We Will Rock You."

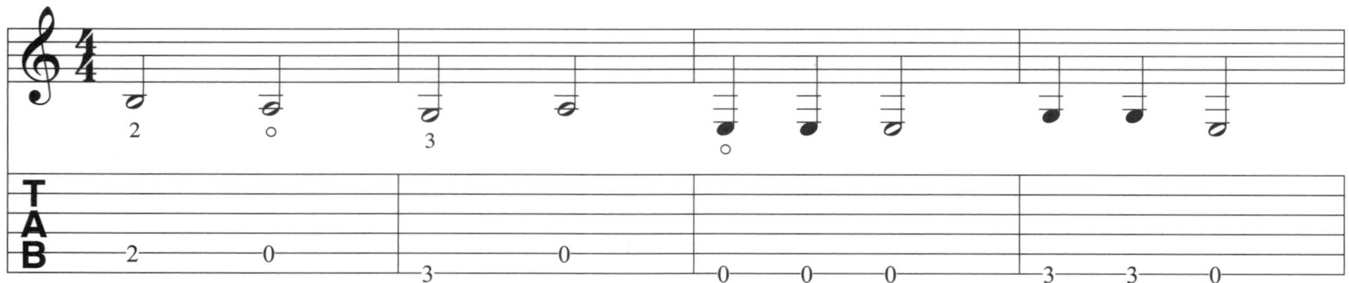

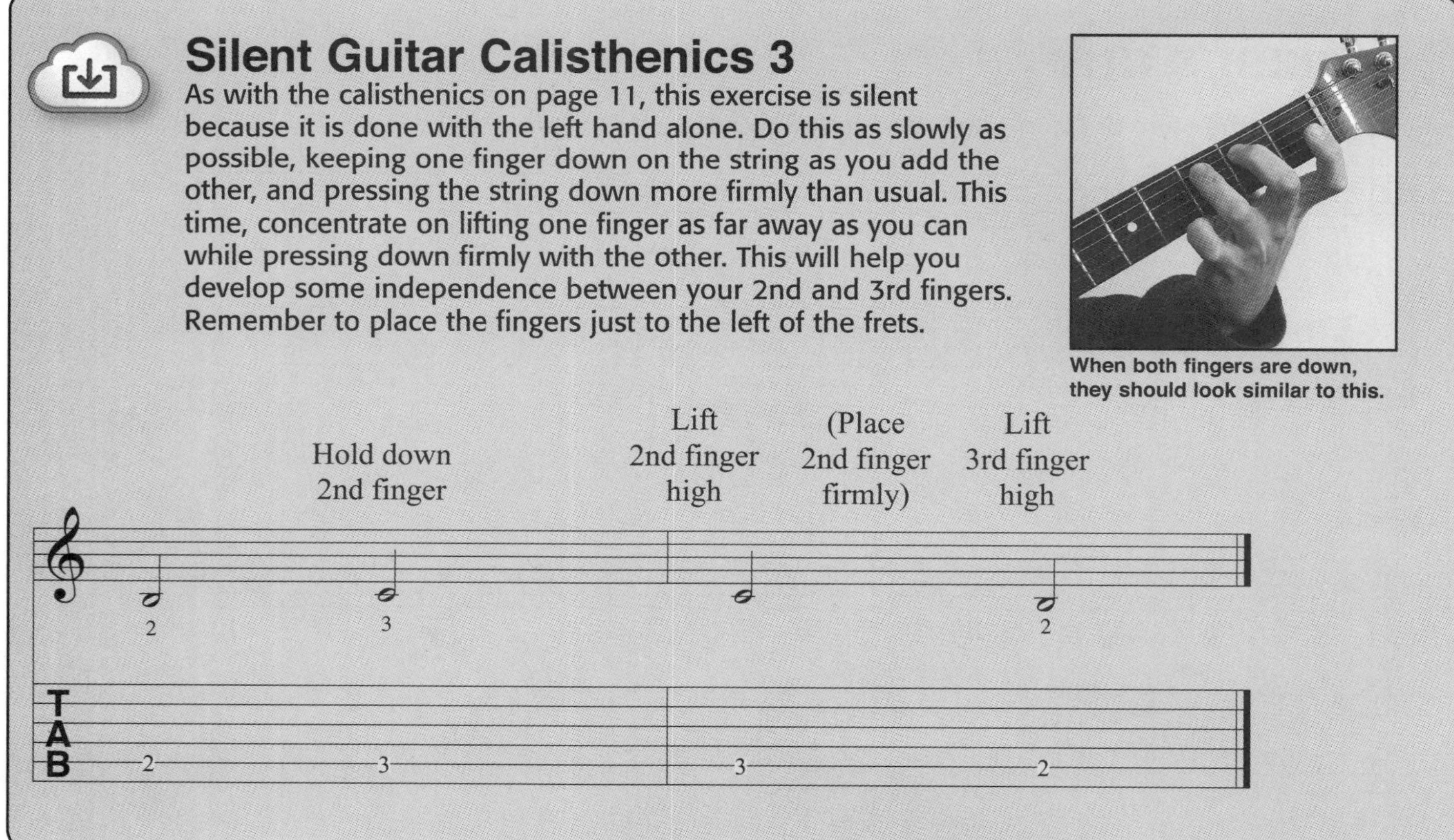

Silent Guitar Calisthenics 3

As with the calisthenics on page 11, this exercise is silent because it is done with the left hand alone. Do this as slowly as possible, keeping one finger down on the string as you add the other, and pressing the string down more firmly than usual. This time, concentrate on lifting one finger as far away as you can while pressing down firmly with the other. This will help you develop some independence between your 2nd and 3rd fingers. Remember to place the fingers just to the left of the frets.

When both fingers are down, they should look similar to this.

NOTES ON THE FOURTH STRING D

4th string,
open

2nd FRET

4th string,
2nd fret

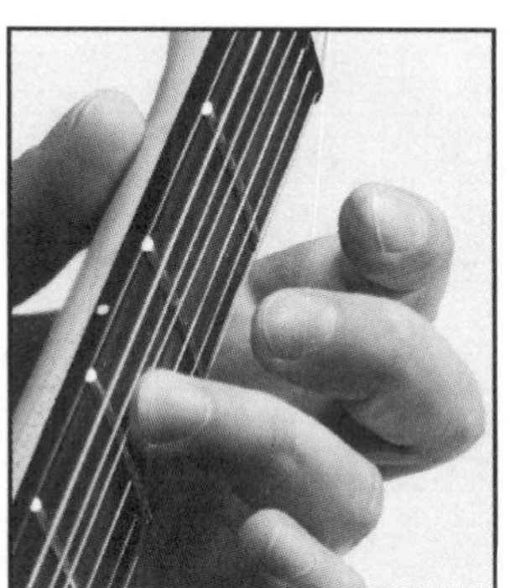

3rd FRET

4th string,
3rd fret

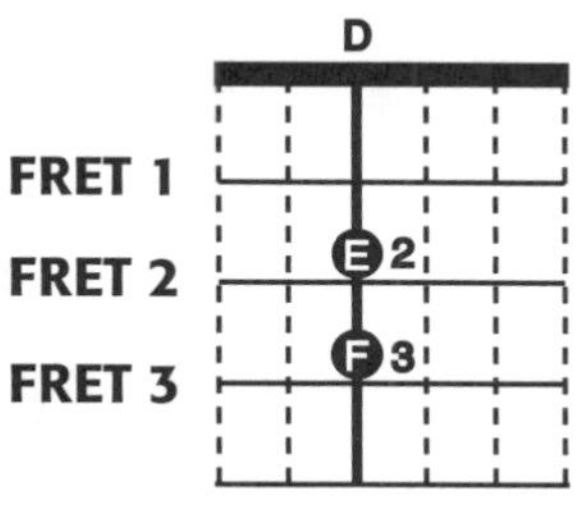

FOURTH-STRING RIFF

1950S ROCK LICK

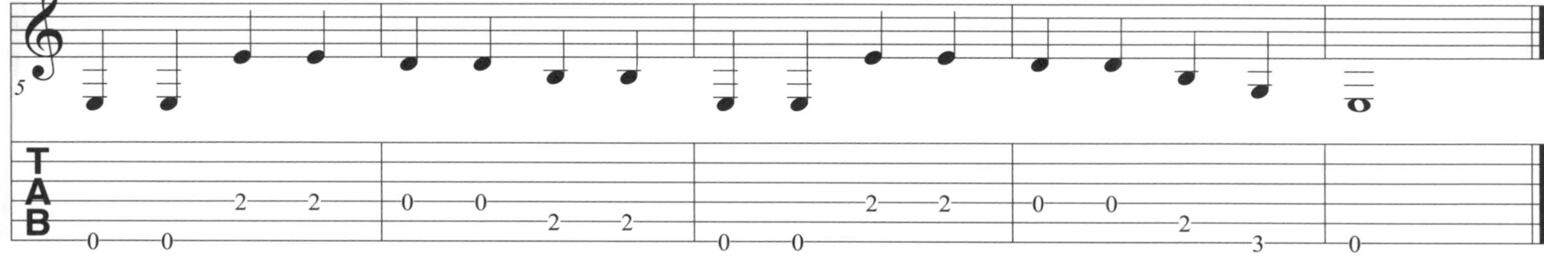

FOGGY LAKE

This next example is in the style of "Smoke on the Water" by the group Deep Purple.

LADDER TO THE SKY

The example below is in the style of one of the most popular rock songs ever, "Stairway to Heaven" by Led Zeppelin.

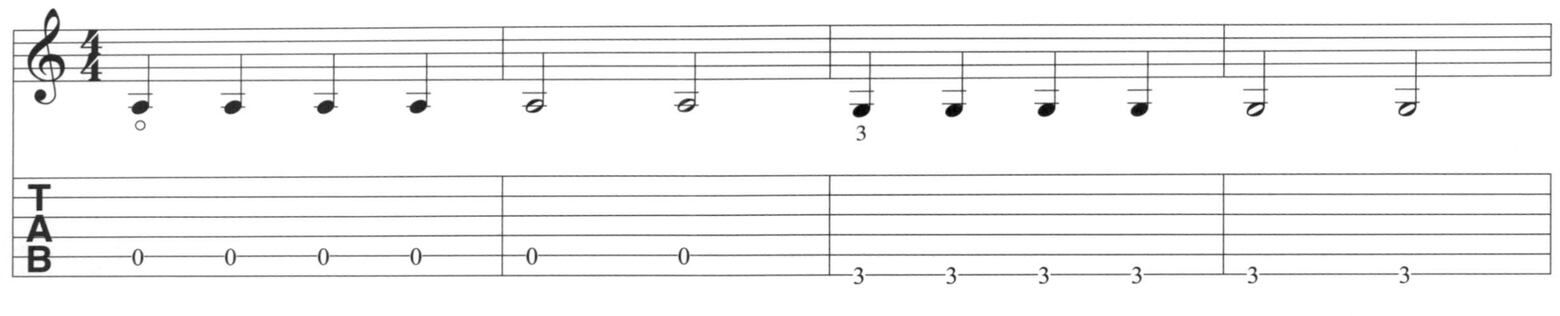

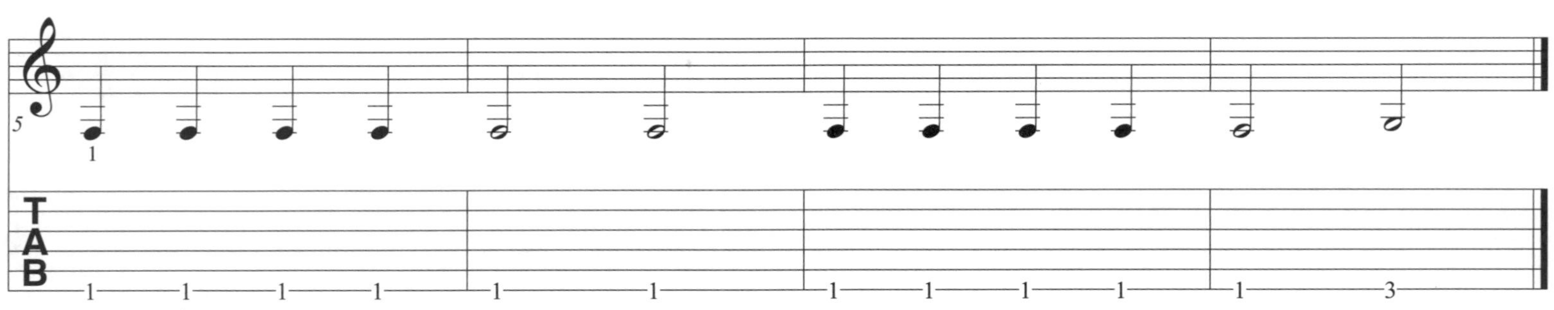

CRAZY KID

This example is in the style of "Wild Child" by The Doors.

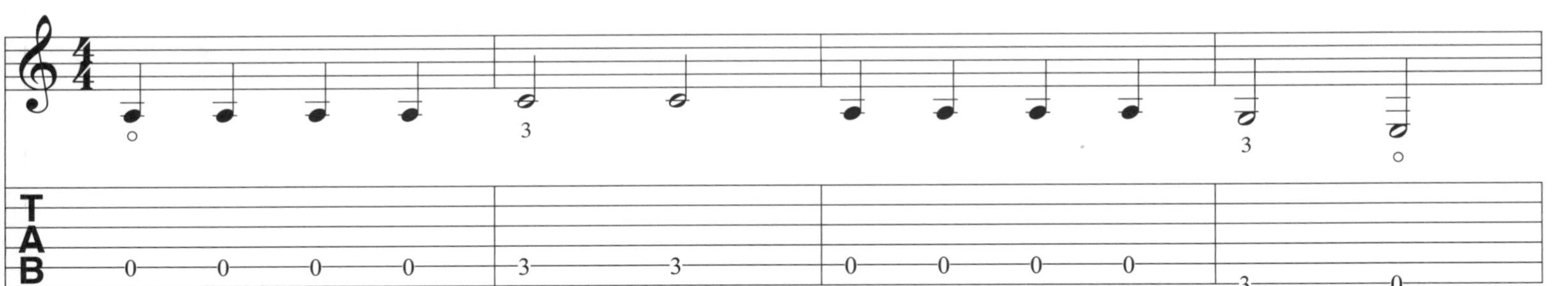

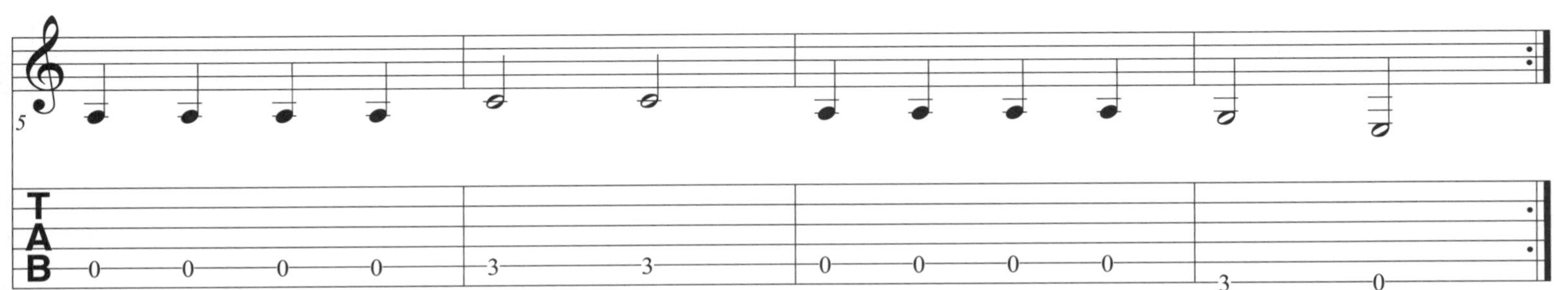

PLAYING TWO NOTES TOGETHER

Until now, you have been playing one note at a time, but in the next example, you will play two notes at once. Make sure to pick the notes quickly so they produce one sound and do not have the effect of two separate notes.

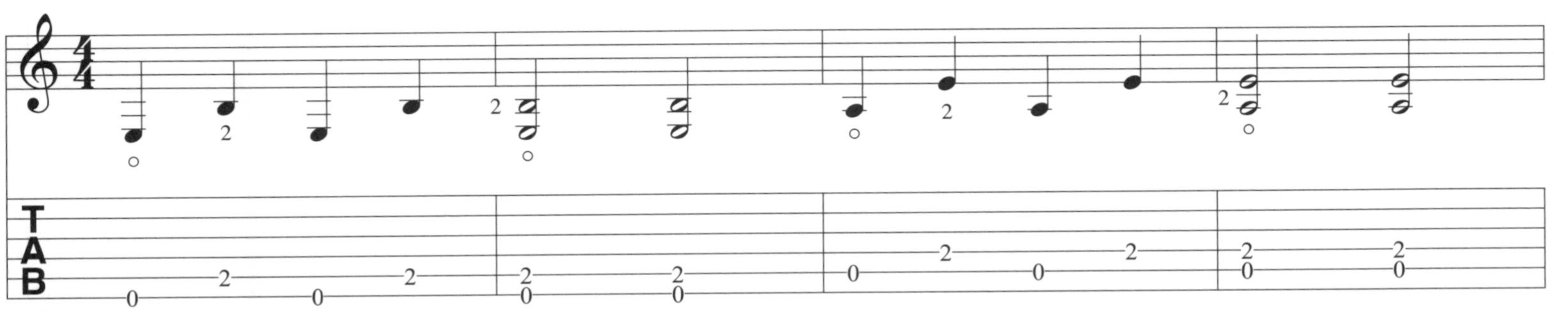

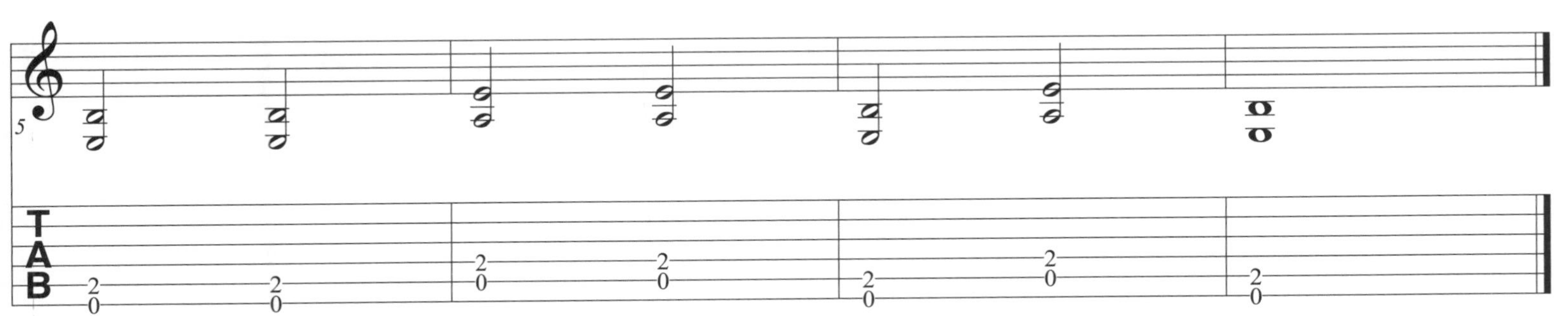

BLUES IN 3

NOTES ON THE THIRD STRING G

OPEN STRING
(not fingered)

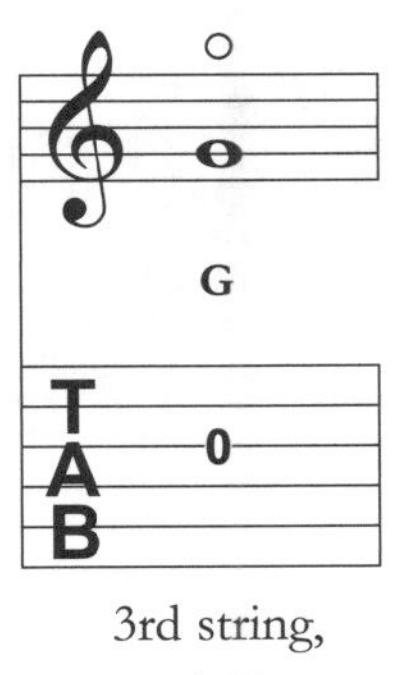

3rd string, open

2nd FRET

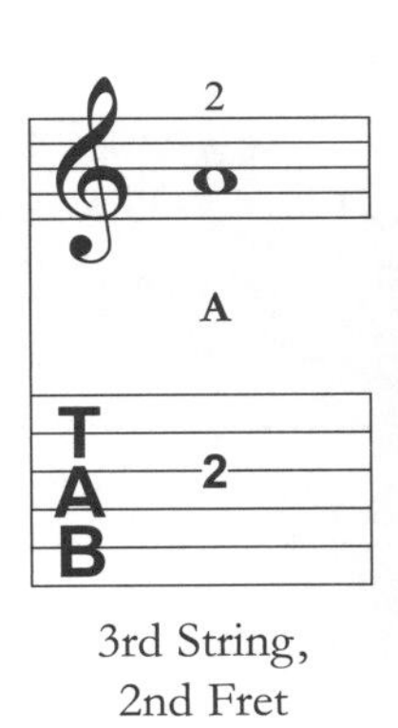

3rd String, 2nd Fret

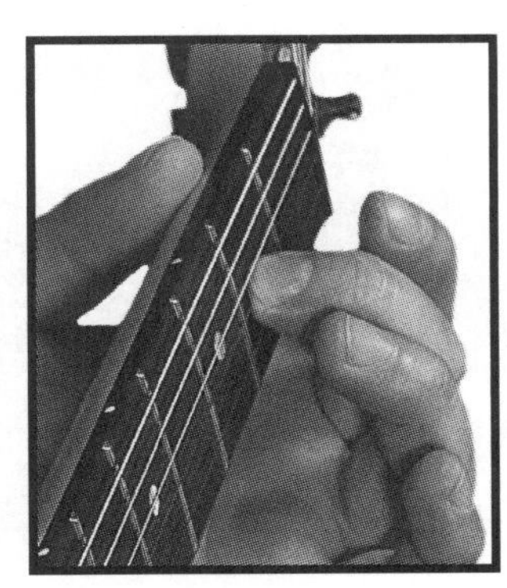

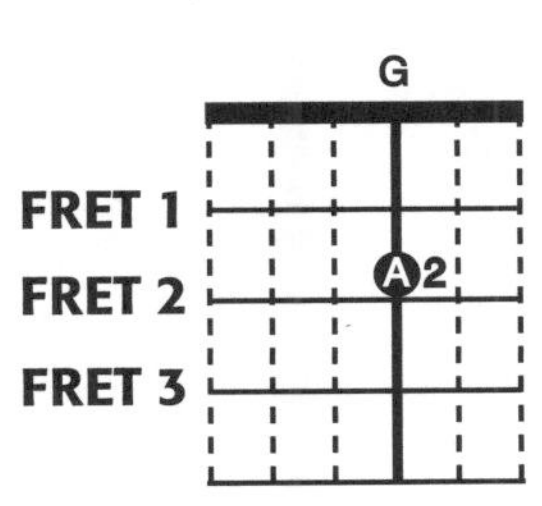

CASH

This example is in the style of "Money" by The Beatles.

Introducing the Quarter Rest

This sign indicates silence for one count. For a clearer effect, you may stop the sound of the strings by touching the strings lightly with the heel of the right hand.

ODE TO JOY

Before Led Zeppelin was formed, Jimmy Page worked as a session musician in recording studios that required him to read music. During that time, he took a few classical guitar lessons to improve his music-reading skills. Classical music spans hundreds of years and thousands of composers, but two of the most famous composers are Beethoven and Bach. Beethoven's "Ode to Joy" is one of the most popular pieces of classical music, and Jimmy plays Bach's "Bouree in E Minor" during "Heartbreaker" on the live album *How the West Was Won*.

ROCKABILLY SOUND

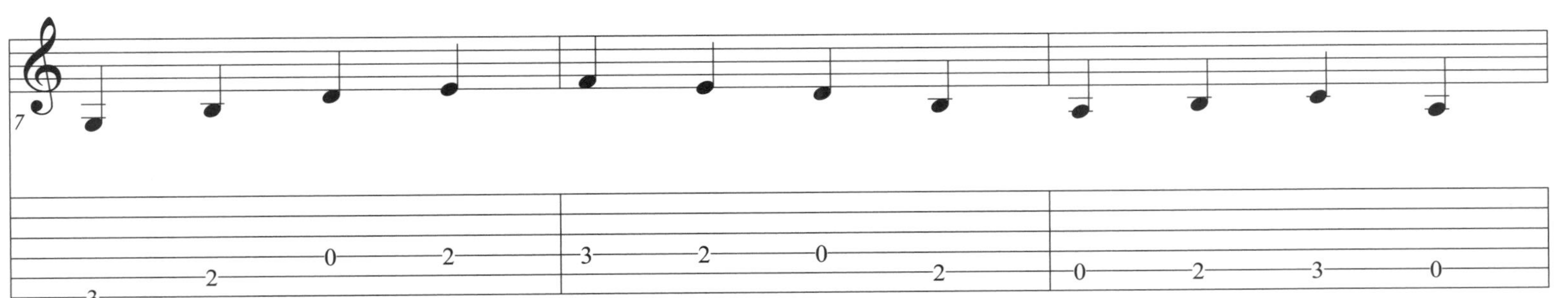

Power Chords

On page 19, you learned to play two notes together. Technically, a chord consists of three or more notes played together, but when you see chords with the symbols A5, D5, or E5 above them, they are special two-note chords called *power chords*. Power chords are some of the most important chords in rock. Add some distortion and play them loud and you will see where they got their name.

THREE-CHORD PROGRESSION

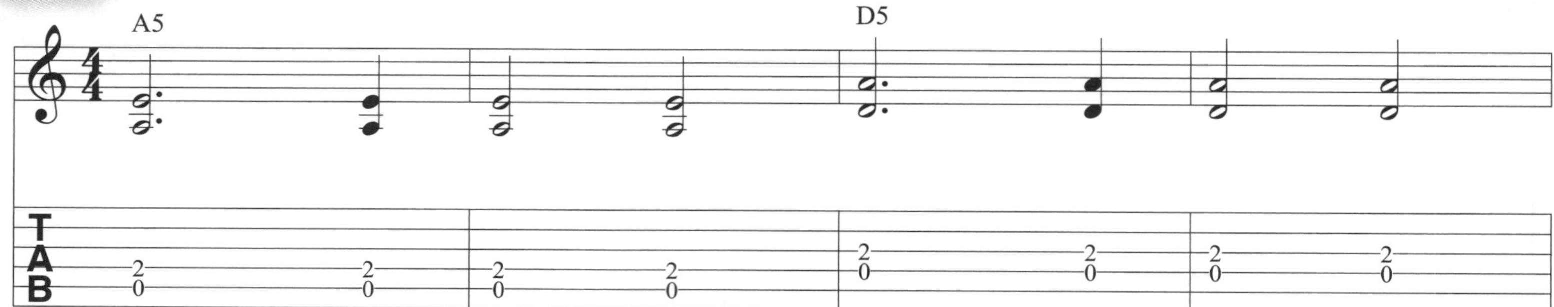

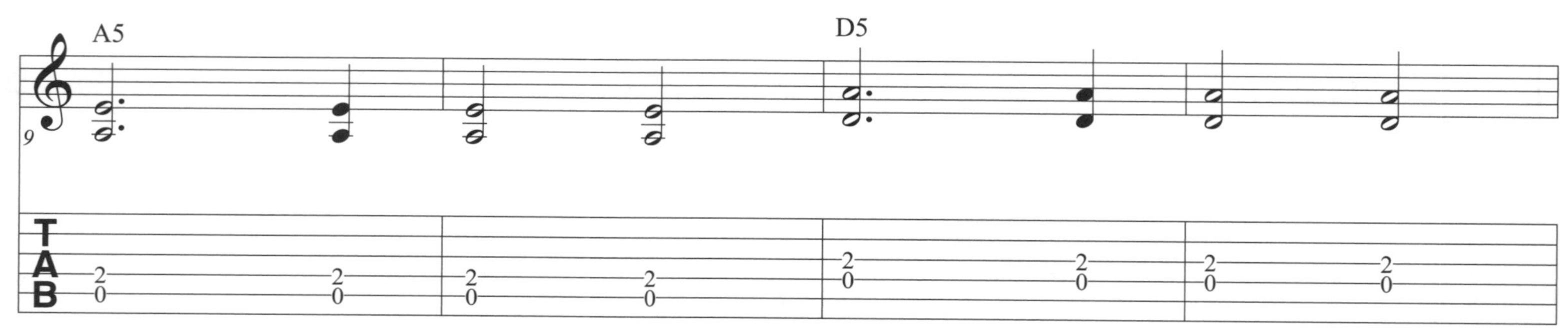

DOWN YOU GO

This example is in the style of "Another One Bites the Dust" by Queen.

REPEAT THE FIRST LINE.

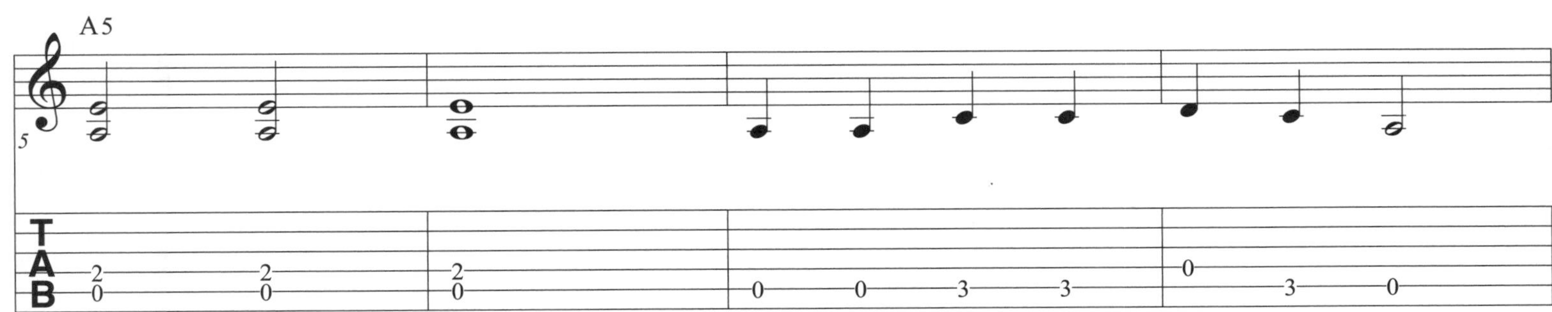

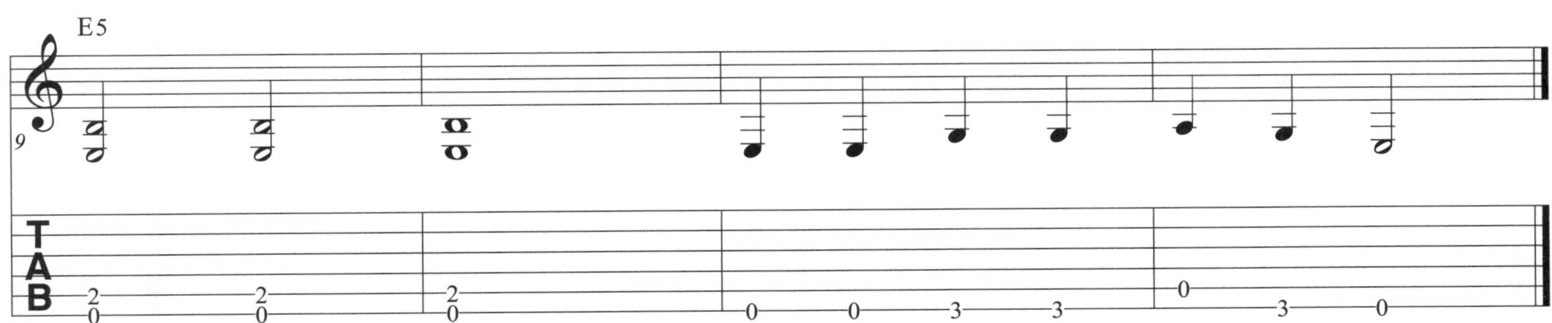

ROCK DUET

This song is a *duet*, which is a piece written for two performers. You can play either the first or second part. Have a teacher or friend accompany you.

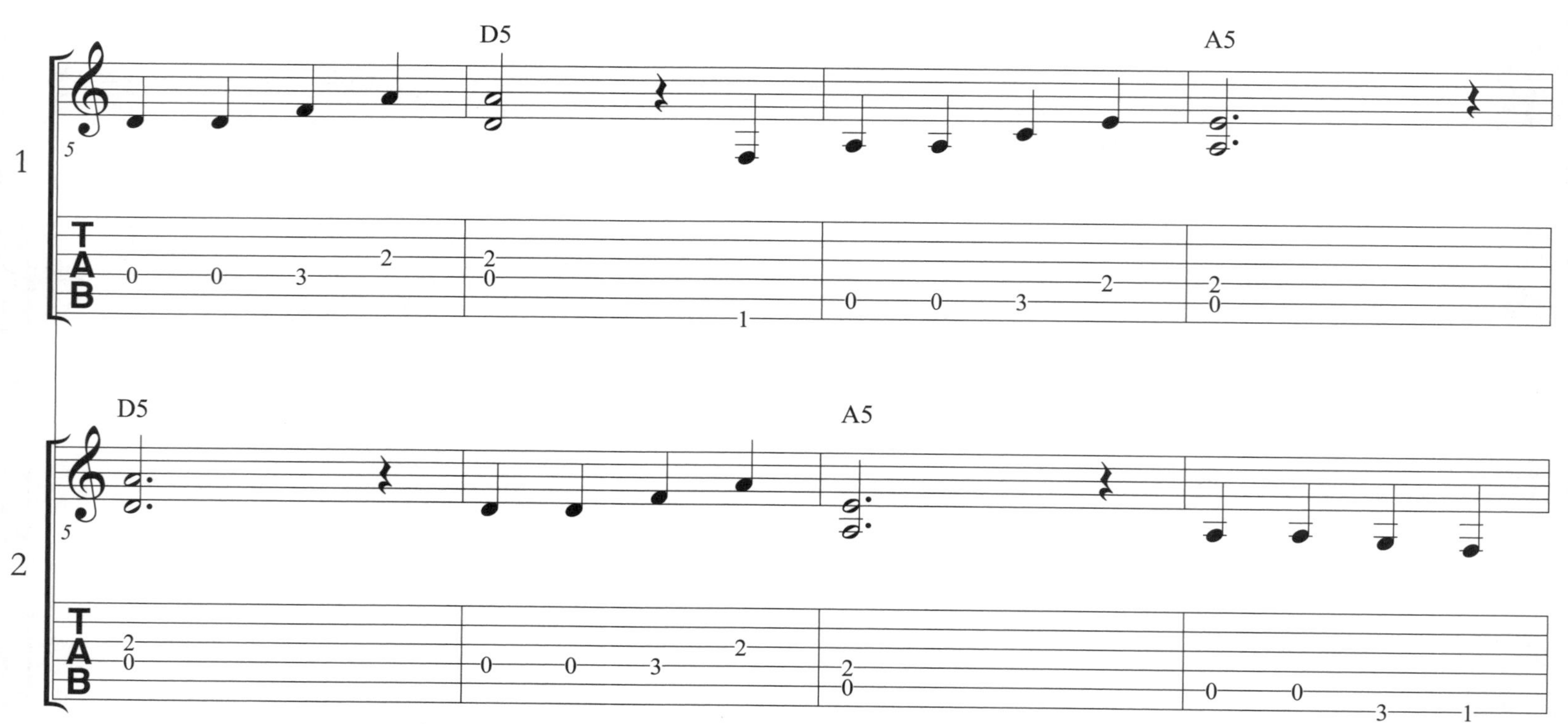

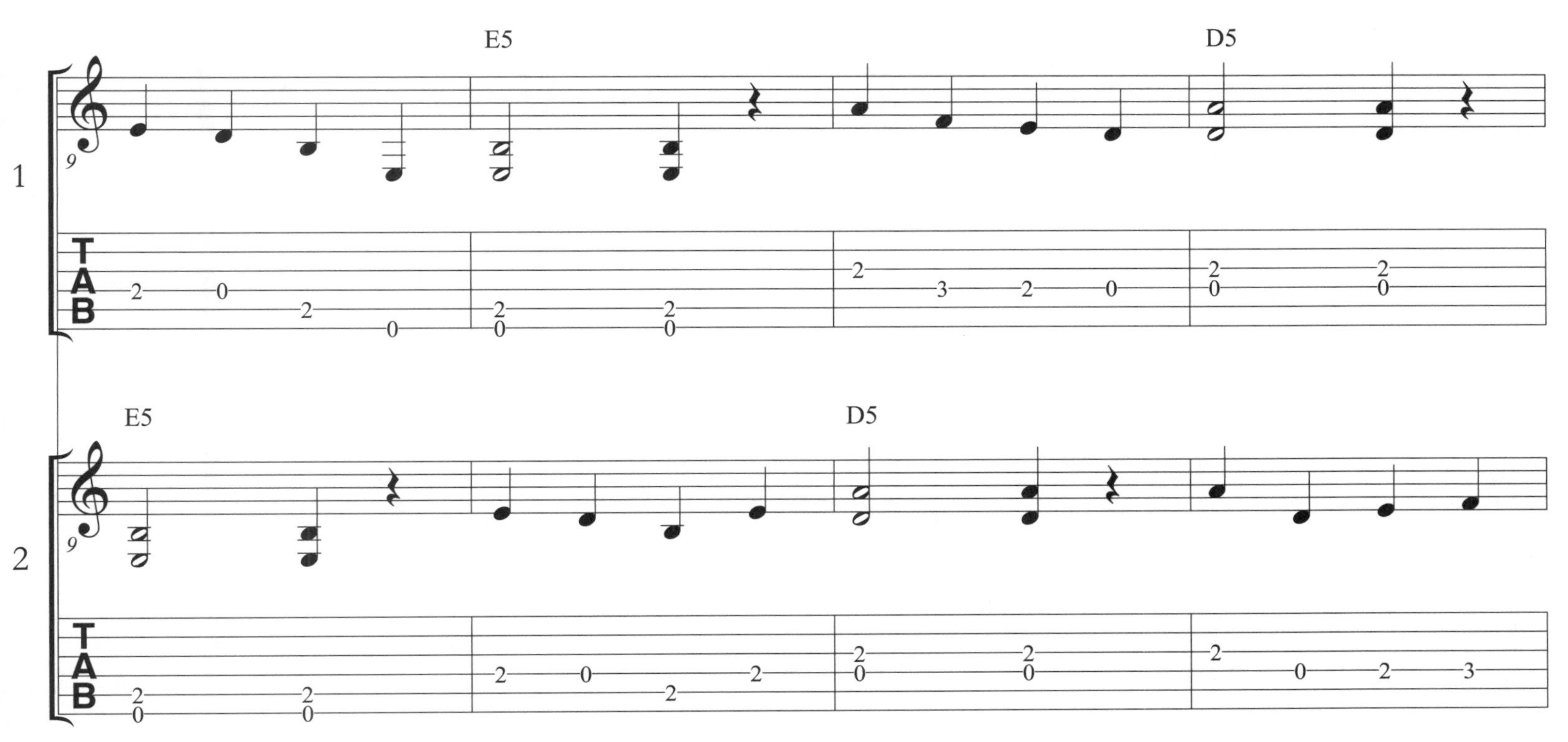
E5
D5
1
9
TAB
2 0 2 0
2 0 2 0
2 3 2 0
2 0 2 0
E5
D5
2
9
TAB
2 0 2 0
2 0 2 2
2 0 2 0
2 0 2 3

E5
1
13
TAB
0 0 3 2
2 0
0 0 3 2
2
A5
A5
2
13
TAB
2 0 2 0 2 0
0 3 0 2
2 0 0 0
0

BOP THE BLITZ

This example is in the style of "Blitzkrieg Bop" by The Ramones.

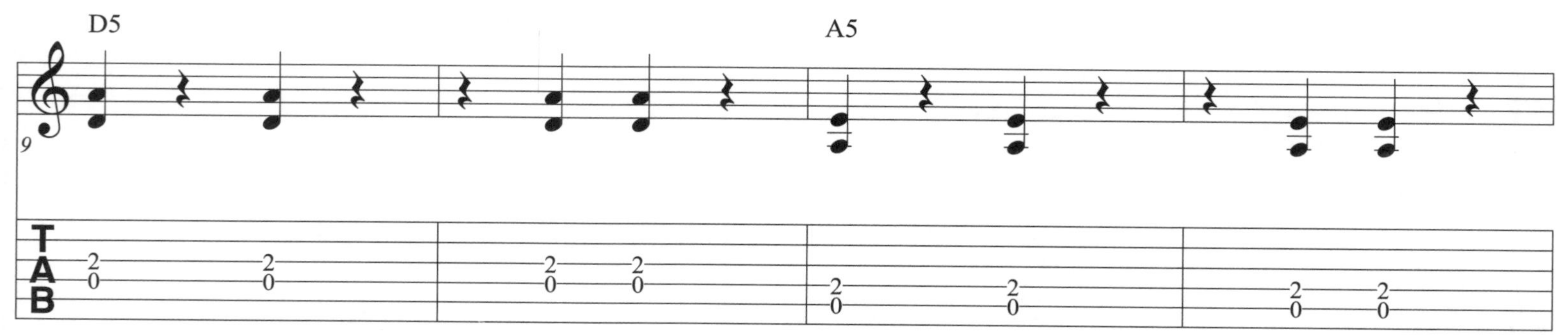

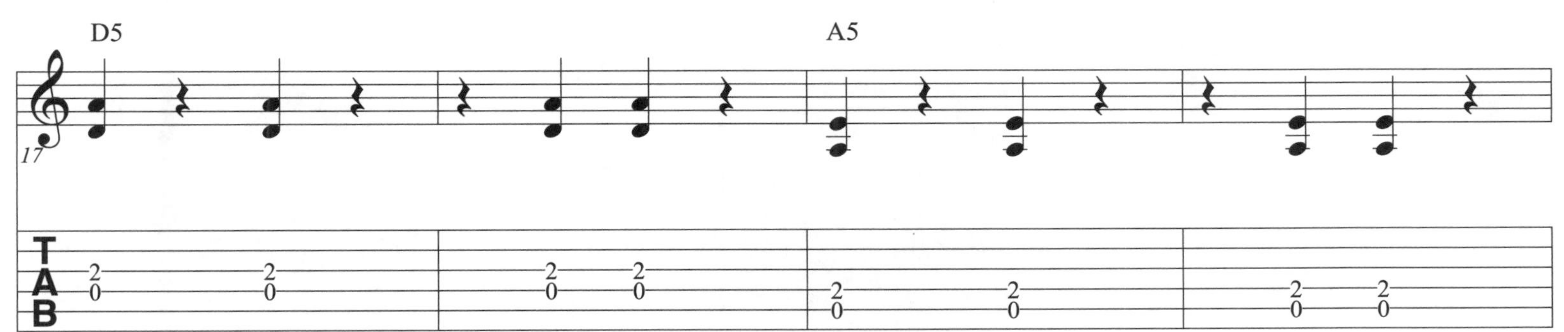
D5
A5
17

E5
A5
21

A5
D5
E5
A5
D5
E5
25

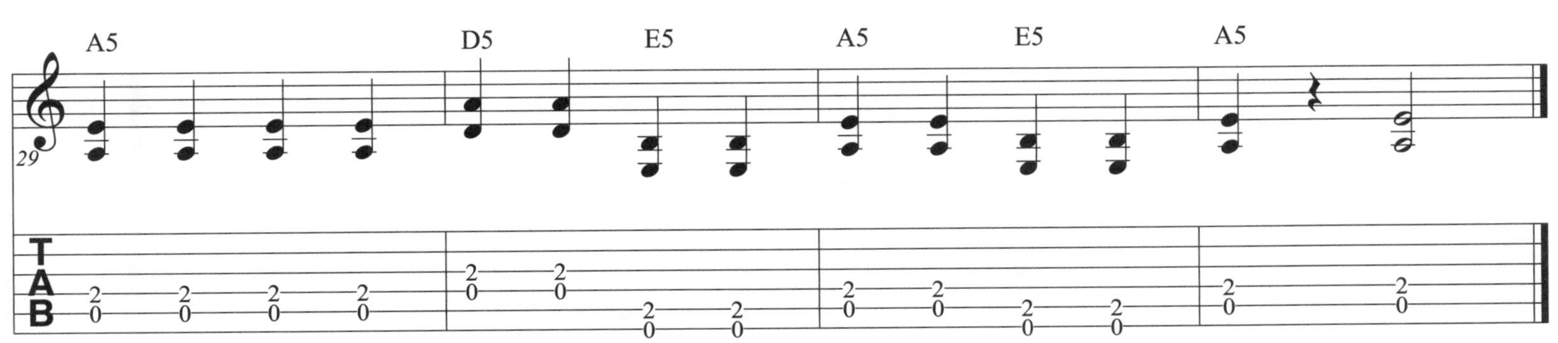
A5
D5
E5
A5
E5
A5
29

NOTES ON THE SECOND STRING B

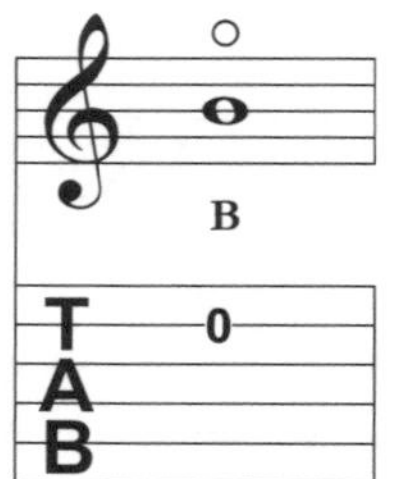

2nd string, open

1st FRET

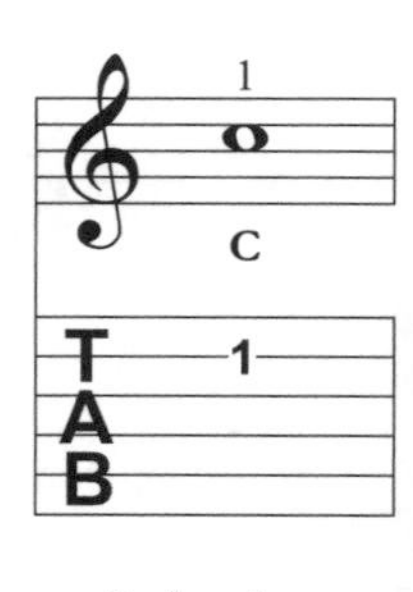

2nd string, 1st fret

3rd FRET

2nd string, 3rd fret

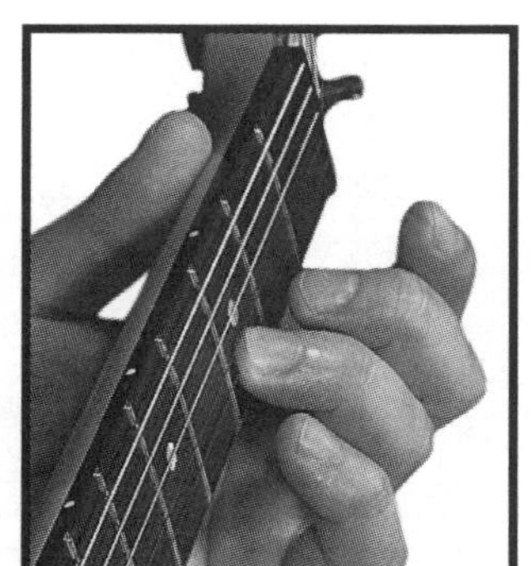

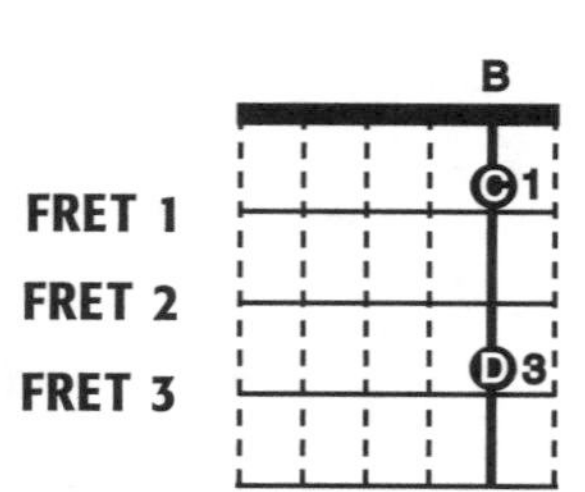

CLASSIC ROCK LICK

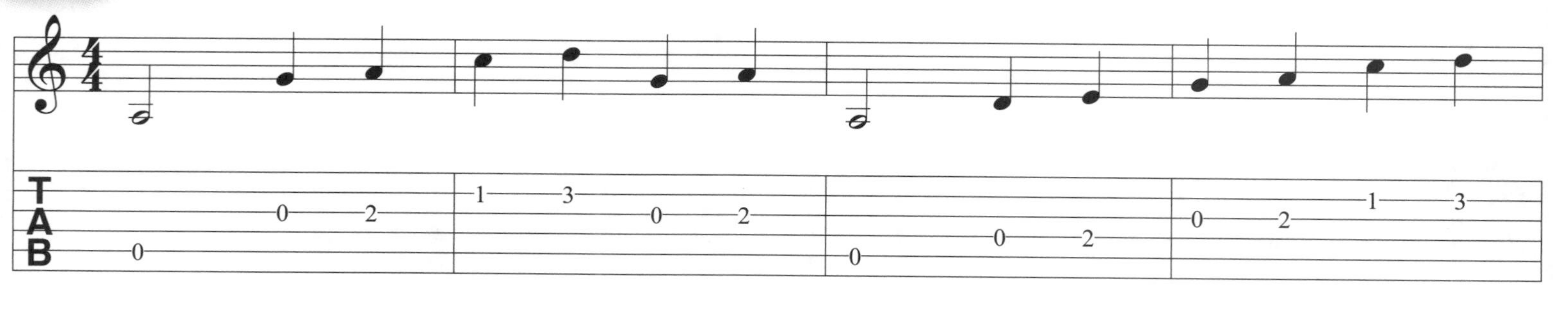

FIVE-STRING ROCK

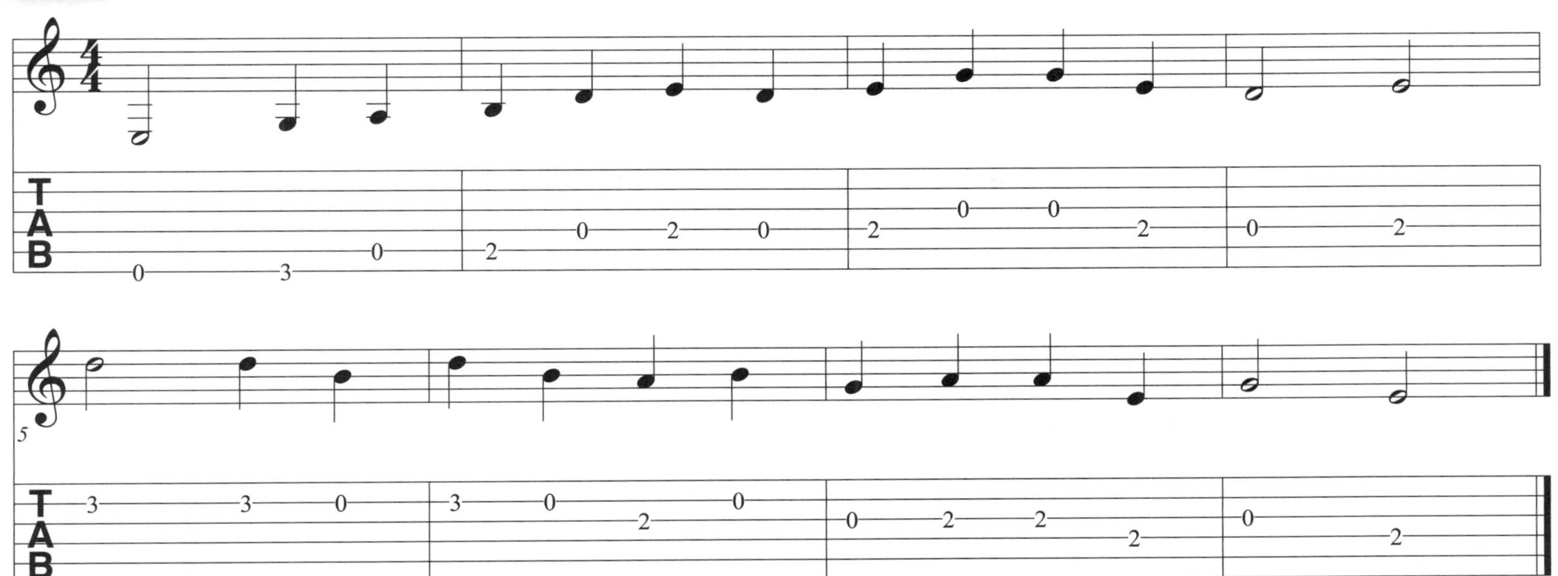

SATISFYING LICK

This example is in the style of “Satisfaction” by The Rolling Stones.

DON'T MISS THE TRAIN

This is in the style of "Last Train to Clarksville" by The Monkees.

GIVE ME A HAND, LADY

This is in the style of "Help Me, Rhonda" by The Beach Boys.

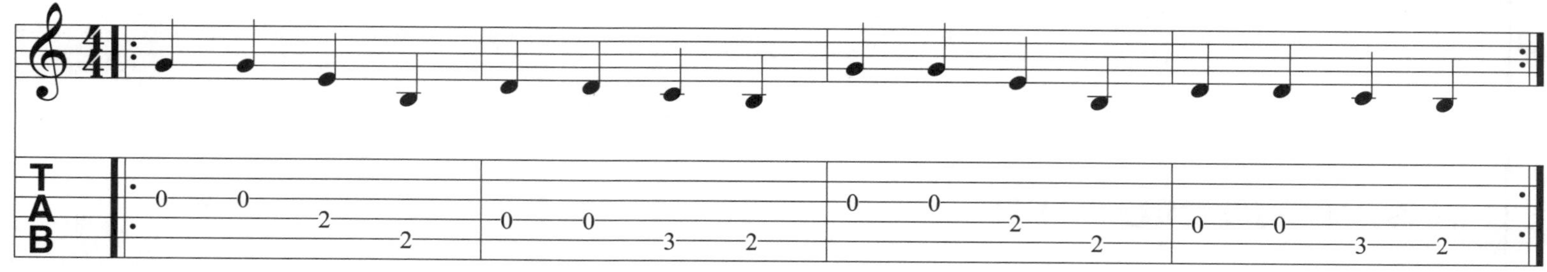

ROCKIN' IN D

NOTES ON THE FIRST STRING E

OPEN STRING
(not fingered)

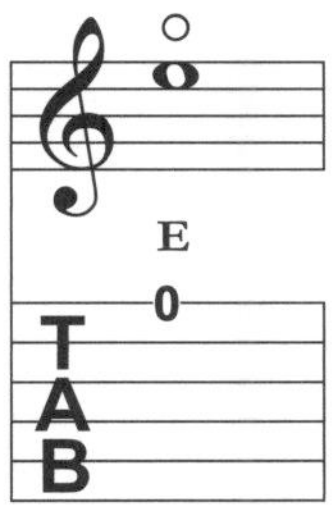

E
0

1st string, open
(not fingered)

1st FRET

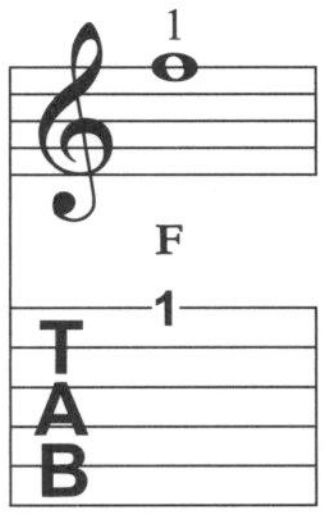

F
1

1st string,
1st fret

3rd FRET

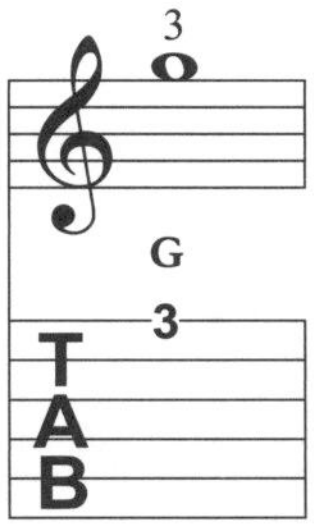

G
3

1st string,
3rd fret

FRET 1
FRET 2
FRET 3

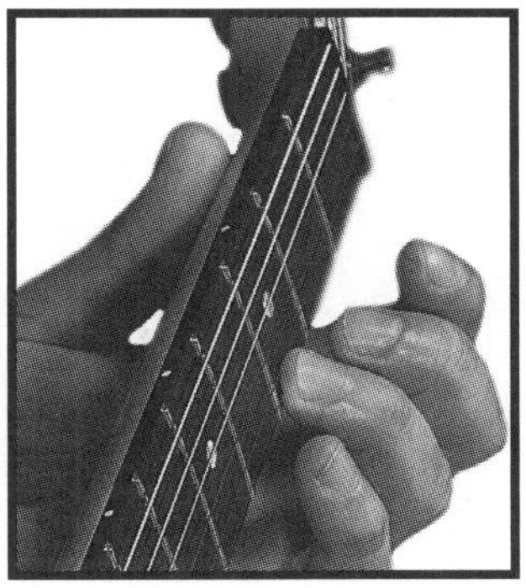

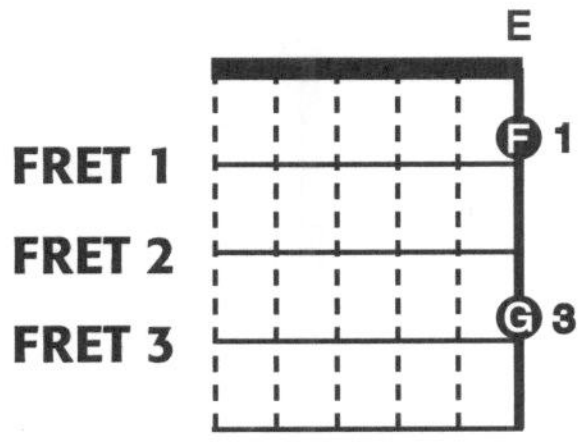

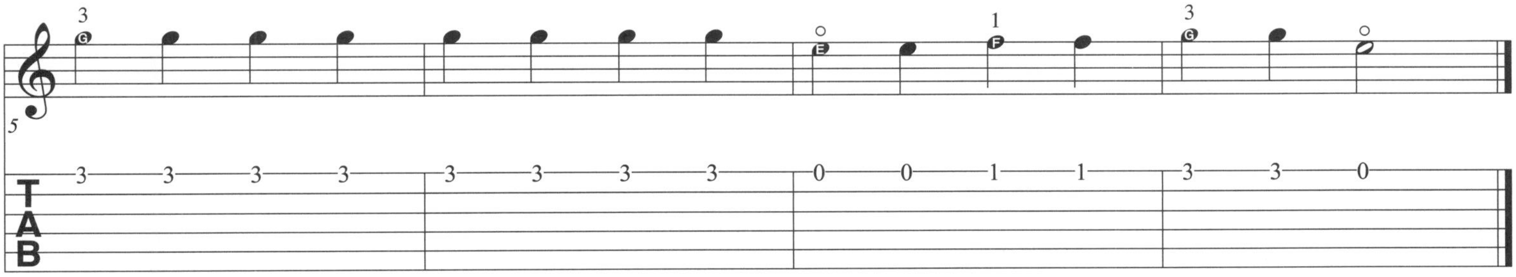

JAMMING WITH E, F, AND G

REVIEW

BASS STRINGS — **SOLO STRINGS**

	6th String	5th String	4th String	3rd String	2nd String	1st String
FRETS:	○ 1 3	○ 2 3	○ 2 3	○ 2	○ 1 3	○ 1 3

E F G A B C D E F G A B C D E F G
T
A
B

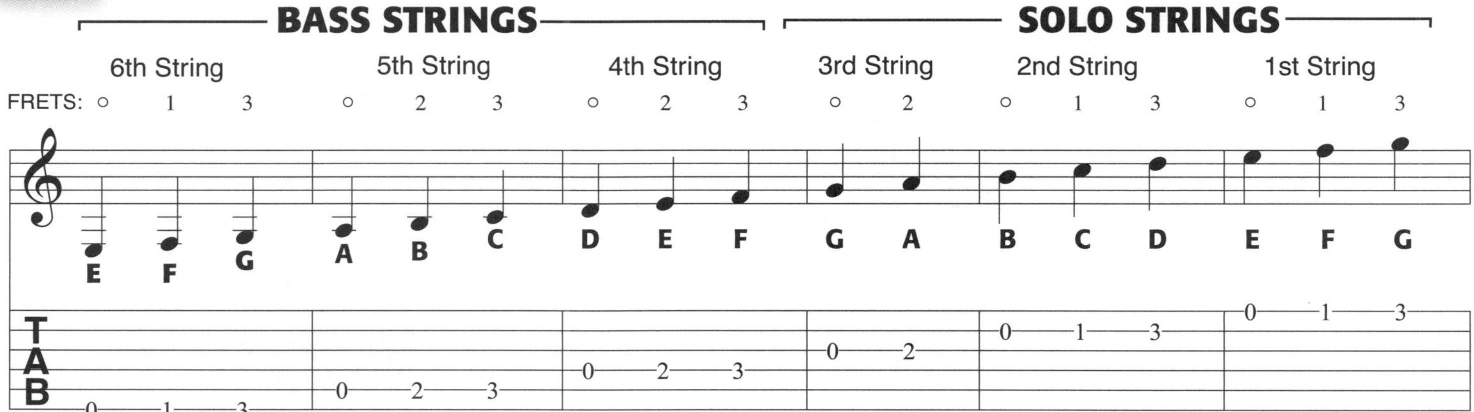

AURA LEE

Elvis Presley recorded this folk song in a modern version called "Love Me Tender."

TEACHER: C
D7
G7
C
C
E7
F
Fm
C
C
A7
D7
G7
C
T
A
B

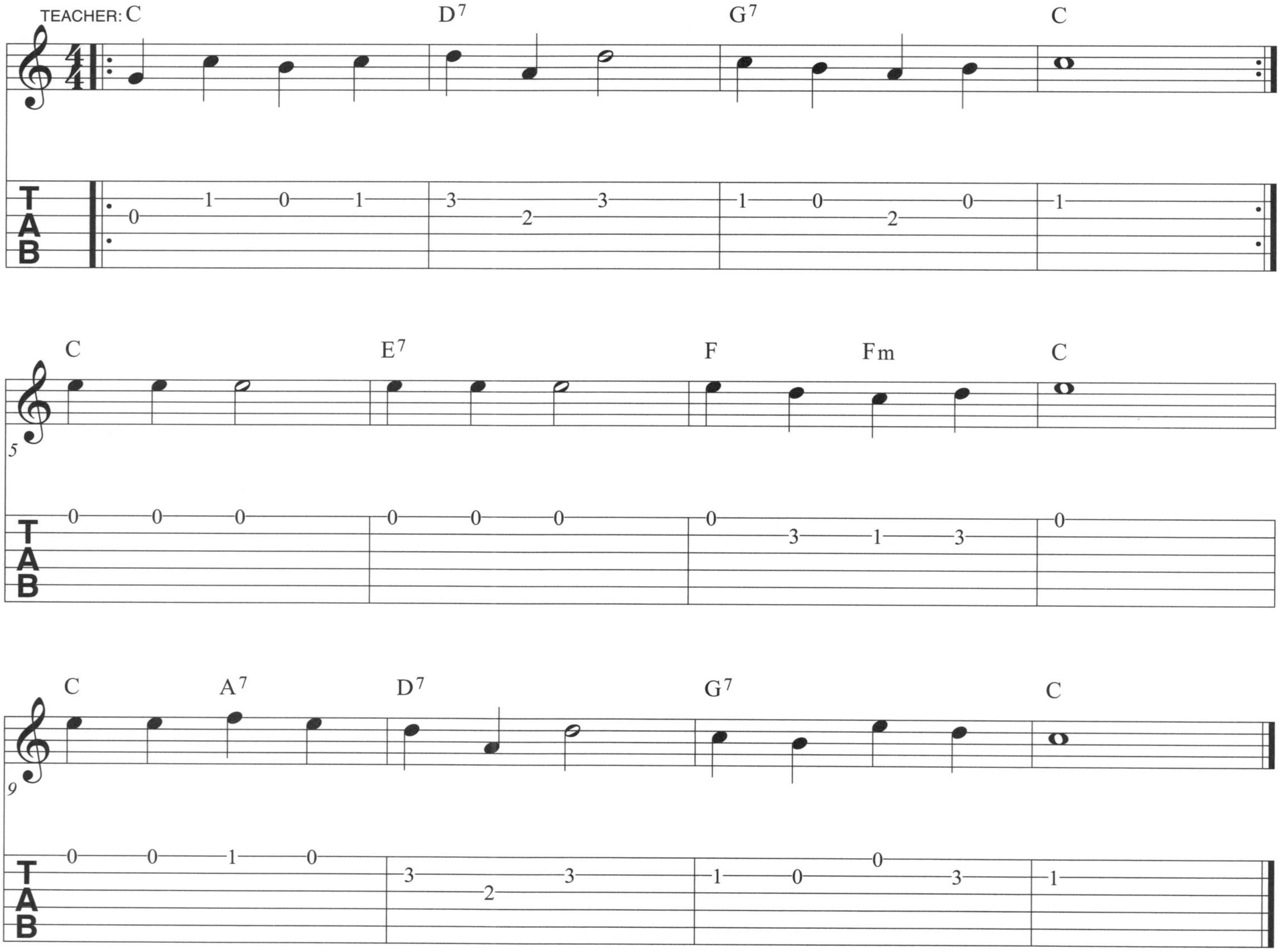

THE MAJOR SCALE

A *major scale* is a specific pattern of eight tones in alphabetical order. The pattern of *whole steps* and *half steps* is what gives the major scale its distinct sound. The distance from one fret to the next fret, up or down, is a half step. Two half steps make a whole step. Following is the pattern of whole steps and half steps for the major scale.

whole step, whole step, half step, whole step, whole step, whole step, half step.

The highest note of the scale, having the same letter name as the first note, is called the *octave* note.

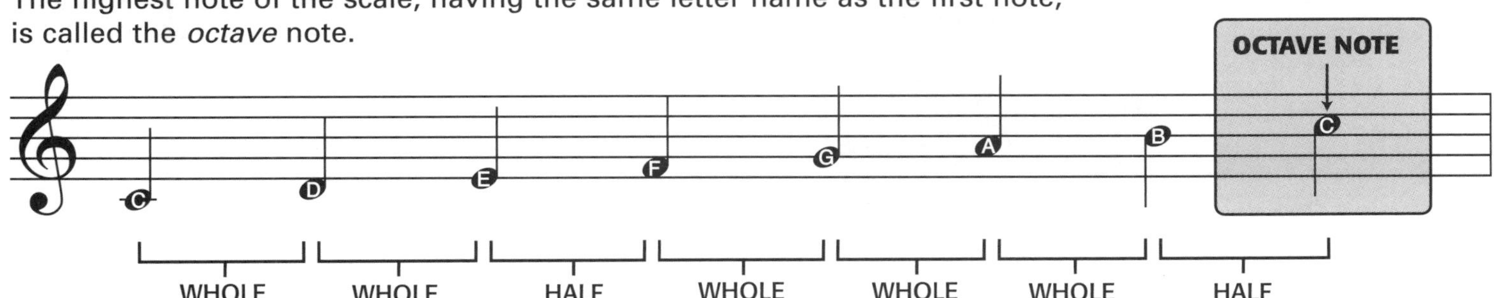

C Major Scale

It is easier to visualize whole steps and half steps on a piano keyboard. Notice there are whole steps between every note except E–F and B–C.

Whole steps—One key between
Half steps—No key between

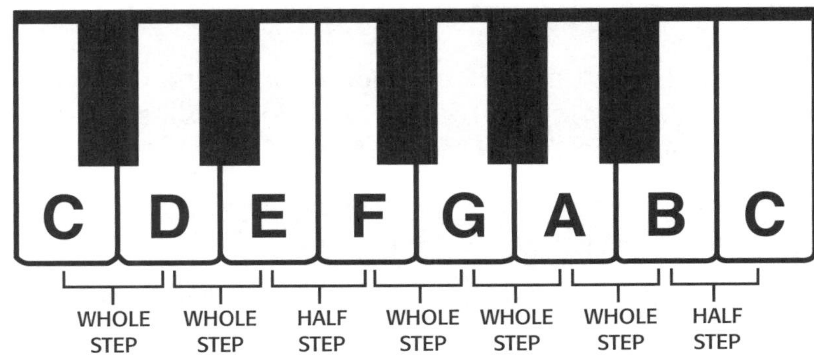

C MAJOR SCALE EXERCISE

SIX-STRING Em CHORD

DO IT YOURSELF: ROCK GUITAR

The lowercase "m" means *minor*. We think of minor chords as having a sad, serious sound.

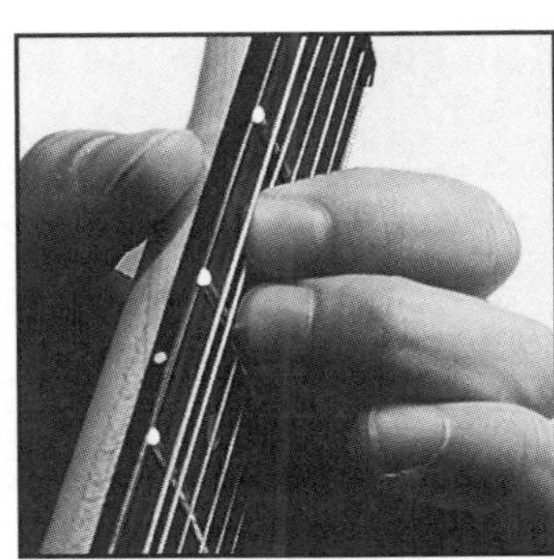

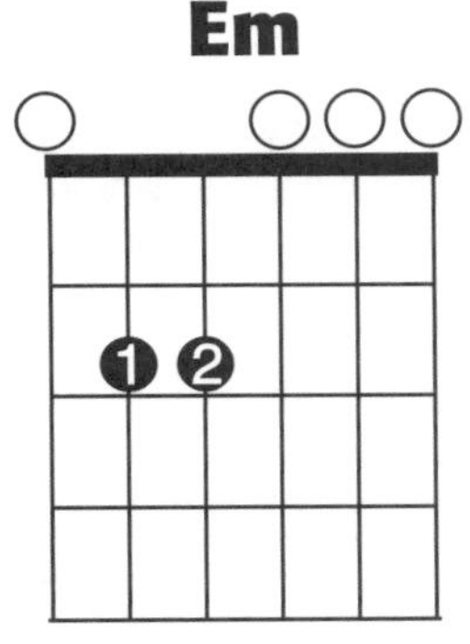

A chord name like C, without an "m" after the letter name, indicates a *major* chord, which has a happier, brighter sound.

Place your 1st and 2nd fingers on the 5th and 4th strings and strum all six strings. This chord can also be played with your 2nd and 3rd fingers.

You learned to strum back on page 4. Since then, you have been strumming two-string power chords. On this page, you are going to be strumming a full six-string Em chord. The "m" in Em stands for "minor," so when you see "Em," you say "E Minor."

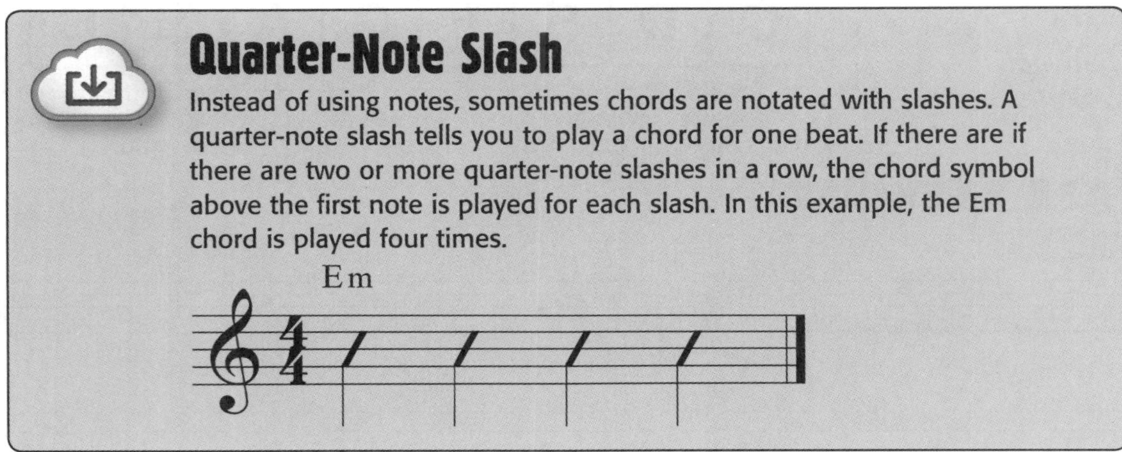

Quarter-Note Slash

Instead of using notes, sometimes chords are notated with slashes. A quarter-note slash tells you to play a chord for one beat. If there are if there are two or more quarter-note slashes in a row, the chord symbol above the first note is played for each slash. In this example, the Em chord is played four times.

Play four measures of the the Em chord. Count out loud and keep the rhythm even. Strum firmly and directly downward across the strings to produce a nice full sound.

Em STRUMMING EXERCISE

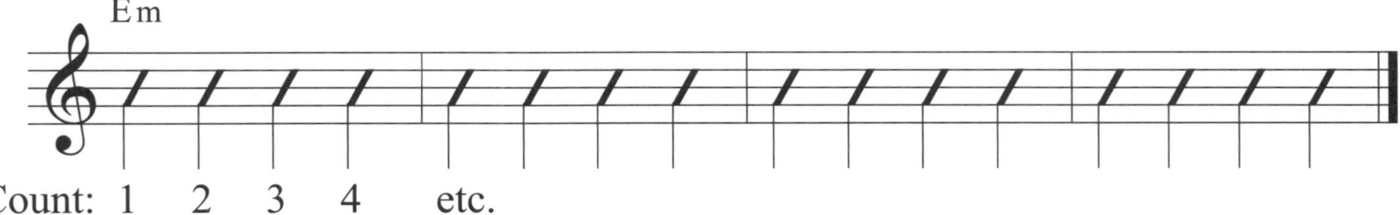

FIVE-STRING A7 CHORD

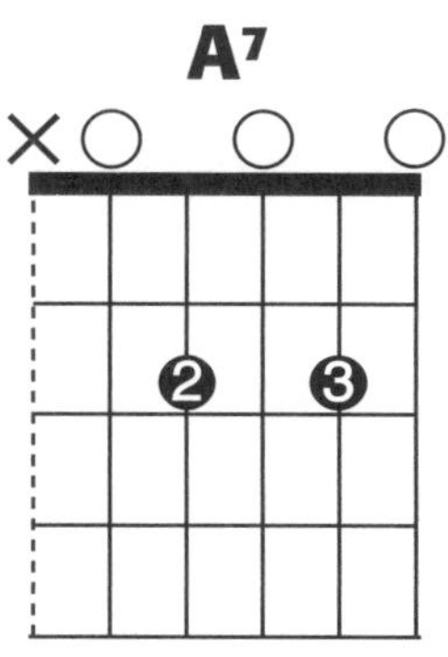

✕ or dashed line = Some sheet music will use an ✕ to show a string not played, but other music will show a dashed line. This book uses both.

Place your 2nd and 3rd fingers on the 4th and 2nd strings, respectively, and only strum the 5th through 1st strings. Unlike the six-string Em chord, you do not strum the 6th string. Instead, you only strum starting on the 5th string. The "7" in A7 stands for "seventh," so when you see "A7," you say either "A Seventh" or "A Seven."

Play four measures of the A7 chord. Count out loud and keep the rhythm even. Remember to strum firmly and directly downward across the strings to produce a nice full sound.

STRUMMING THE A7 CHORD

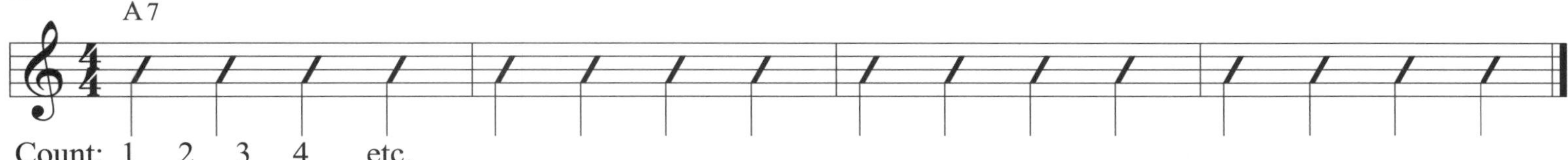

In this example, you are changing chords in each measure. Since both chords are played using the 2nd finger on the 4th string at the 2nd fret, you need only lift the 1st finger and place the 3rd finger. Play it slowly at first, and as you change chords, lift and place the two fingers smoothly and at exactly at the same time. Gradually increase the speed as you become more comfortable changing chords.

STRUMMING Em AND A7 CHORDS

MINOR TWO-CHORD ROCK

This tune uses the two chords you know, along with single notes and rests. Even when there are rests, you continue to play the same chord until a new chord symbol is used. In the last two measures, you change quickly from Em to A7 and back. Practice just those two measures slowly until you can change chords in time, and then play the entire tune.

INTRODUCING HIGH A

DO IT YOURSELF: ROCK GUITAR

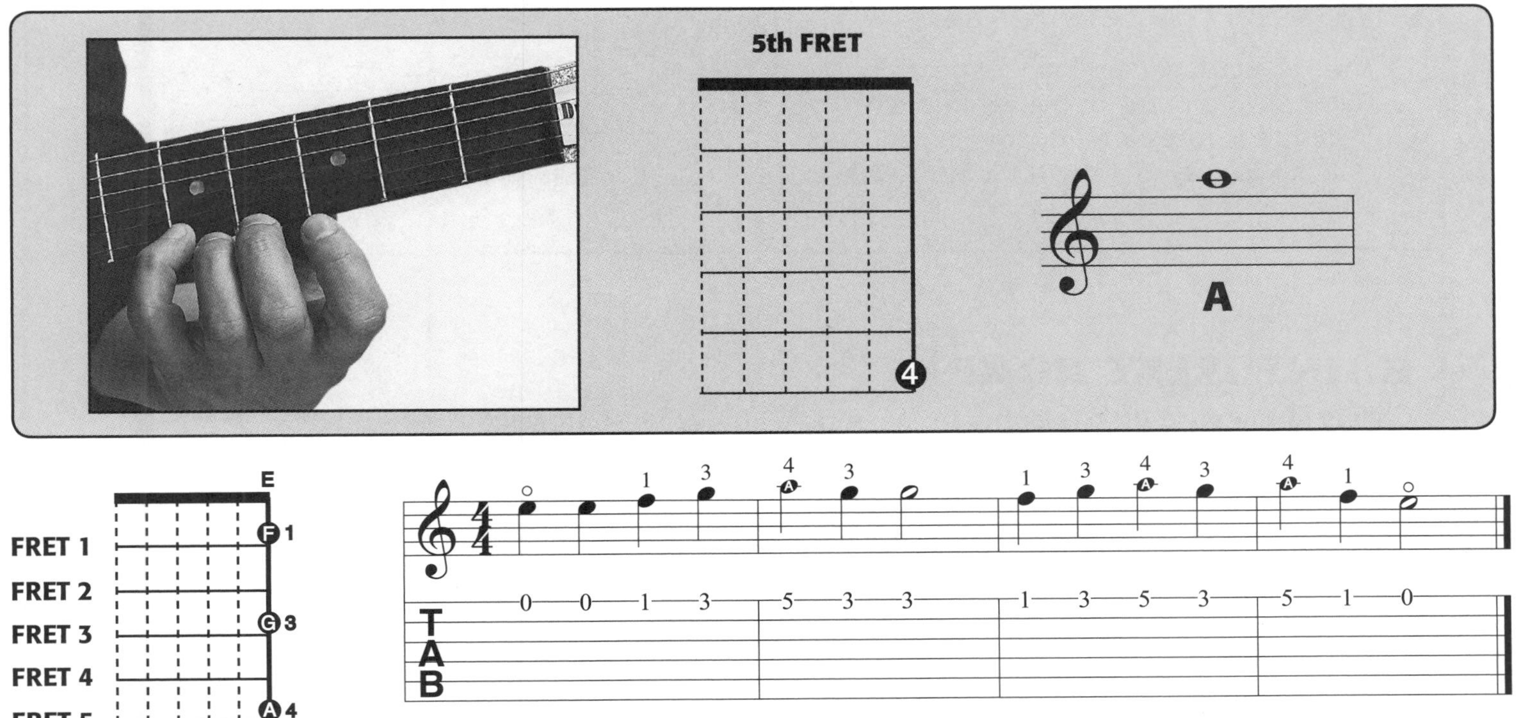

FRET 1 — F 1
FRET 2
FRET 3 — G 3
FRET 4
FRET 5 — A 4

A *mode* is a type of scale that uses the notes of another scale, such as the major scale (page 35), in a different order. The Dorian mode uses the notes of the C Major scale starting on D instead of C.

ROCKIN' IN DORIAN MODE

TEACHER: Dm

Dm | C | Dm

Dm | C | Dm

Dm | A7 | | Dm

Ties

A *tie* is a curved line that connects two or more notes of the same pitch. When two notes are tied, the second one is not played; rather, the value is added to the first note.

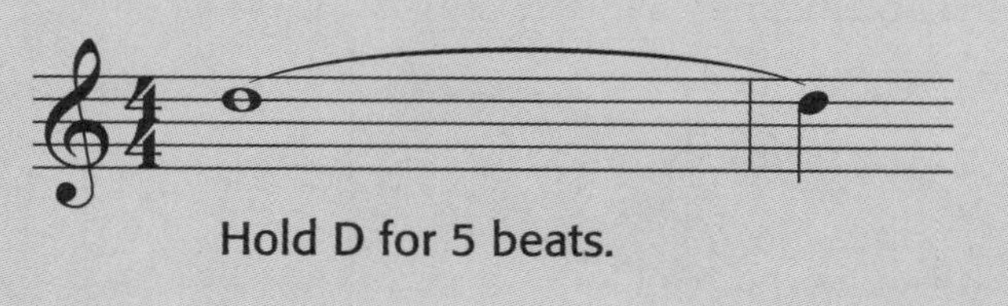

Hold D for 5 beats.

RAINFOREST ROMP

This is in the style of "Welcome to the Jungle" by Guns N' Roses.

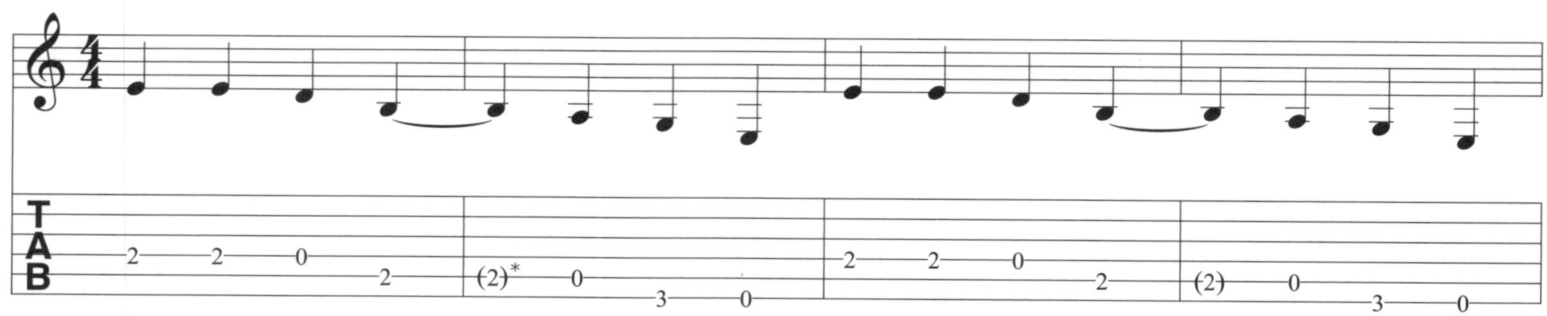

* In TAB, a tied note is shown in parentheses.

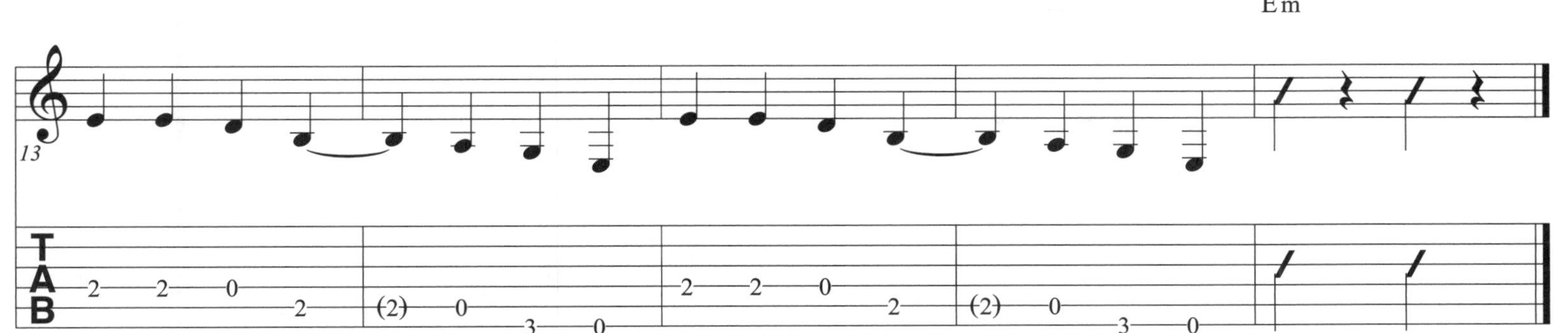

NICE ATTIRE

This is in the style of "Sharp Dressed Man" by ZZ Top.

EIGHTH NOTES

Eighth notes are black notes with a flag added to the stem:

Two or more eighth notes are written with beams:
Each eighth note receives one half beat.

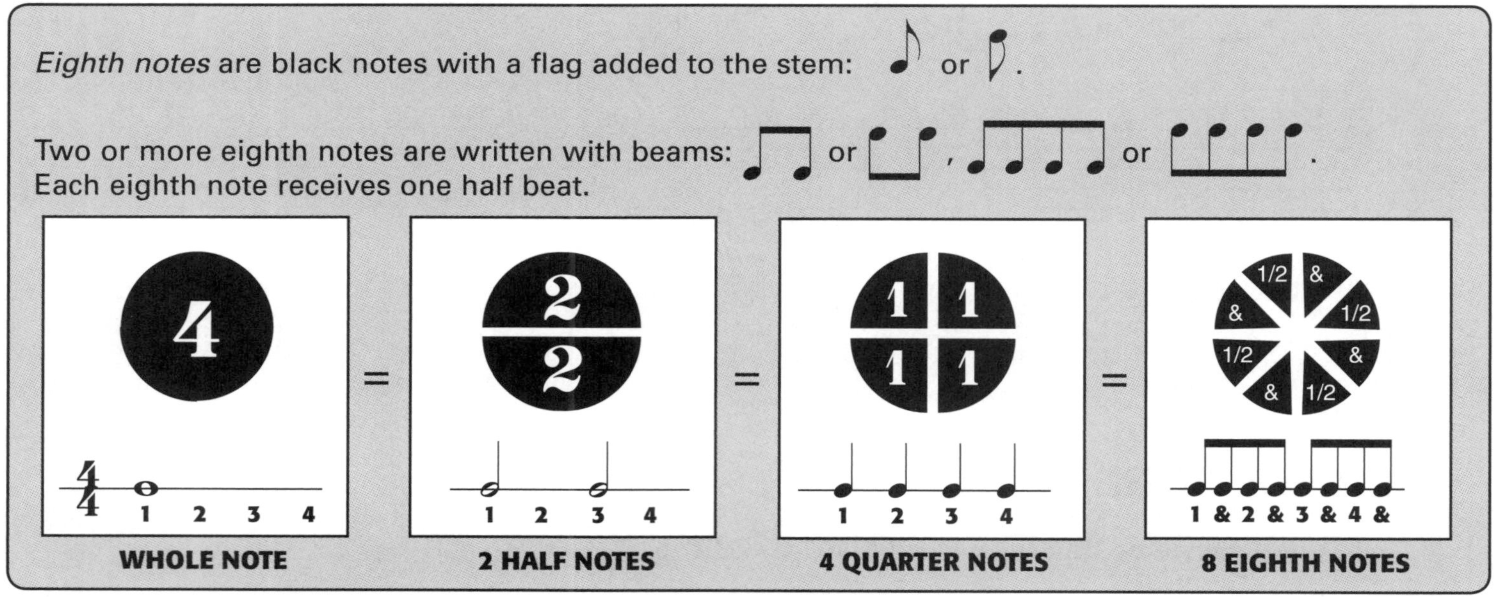

Use alternating down-strokes ⊓ and up-strokes V on eighth notes.

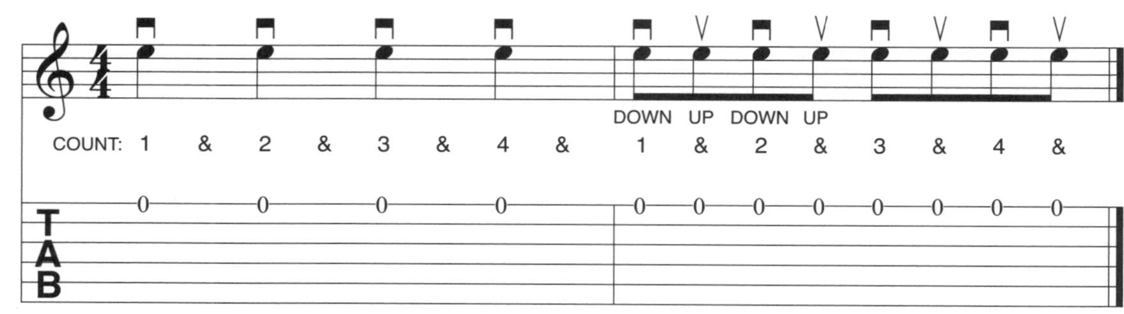

EIGHTH-NOTE EXERCISE

ELLIS ISLAND

This is in the style of "Immigrant Song" by Led Zeppelin.

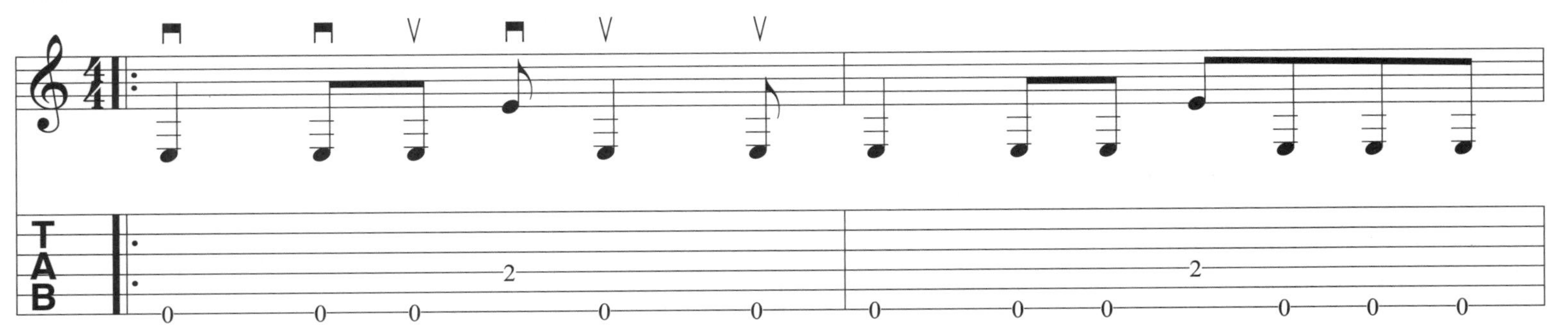

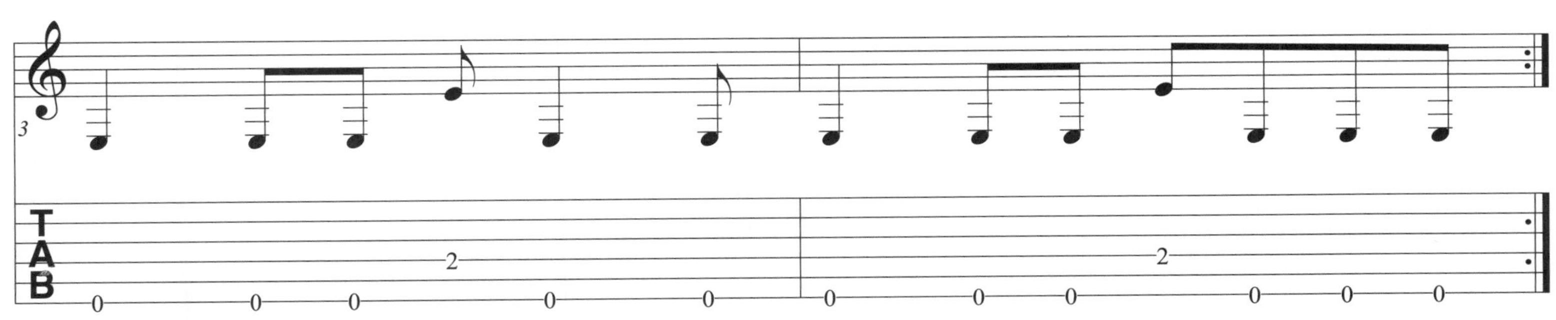

FOUR-STRING D7 CHORD

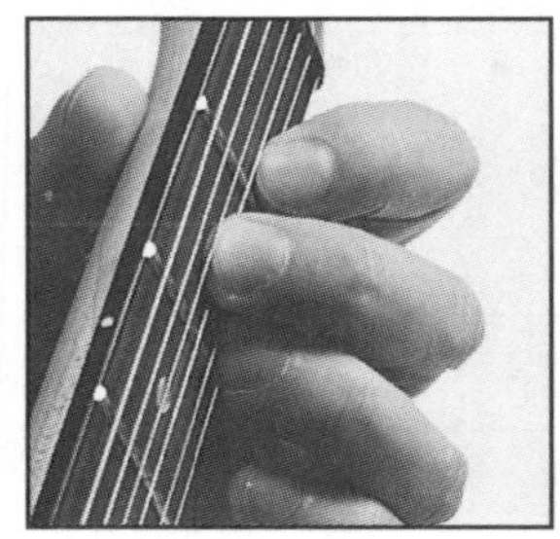

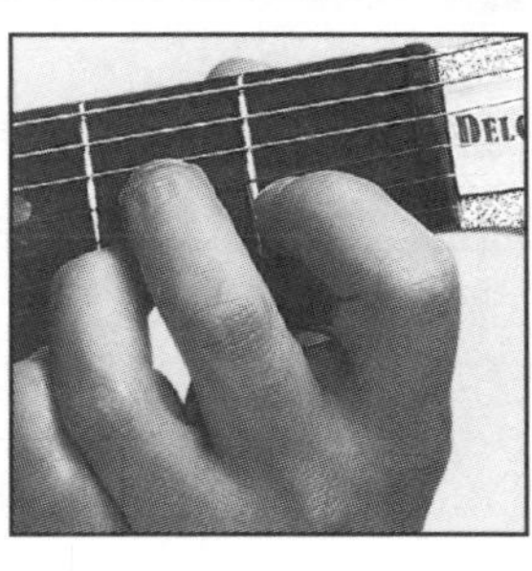

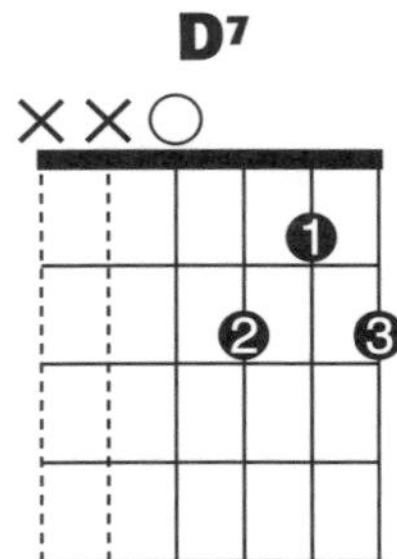

This chord uses three fingers. Place your 1st finger on the 2nd string, 1st fret, and 2nd and 3rd fingers on the 3rd and 1st strings. Only strum the 4th through 1st strings. Do not strum the 5th or 6th strings. Play four measures of the D7 chord. Count out loud and keep the rhythm even. Remember to strum firmly and directly downward across the strings to produce a nice full sound.

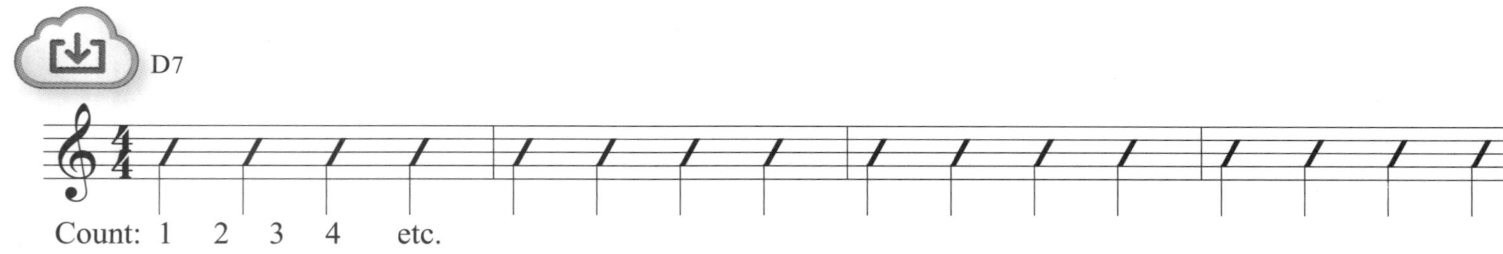

D7 AND A7 CHORD EXERCISE

Remember to practice the changes slowly, and then gradually increase the speed as you become more comfortable changing chords.

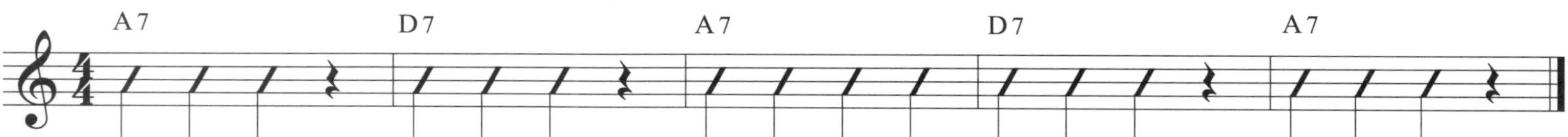

D7 CHORD WITH NOTES

This example combines the D7 chord with single notes.

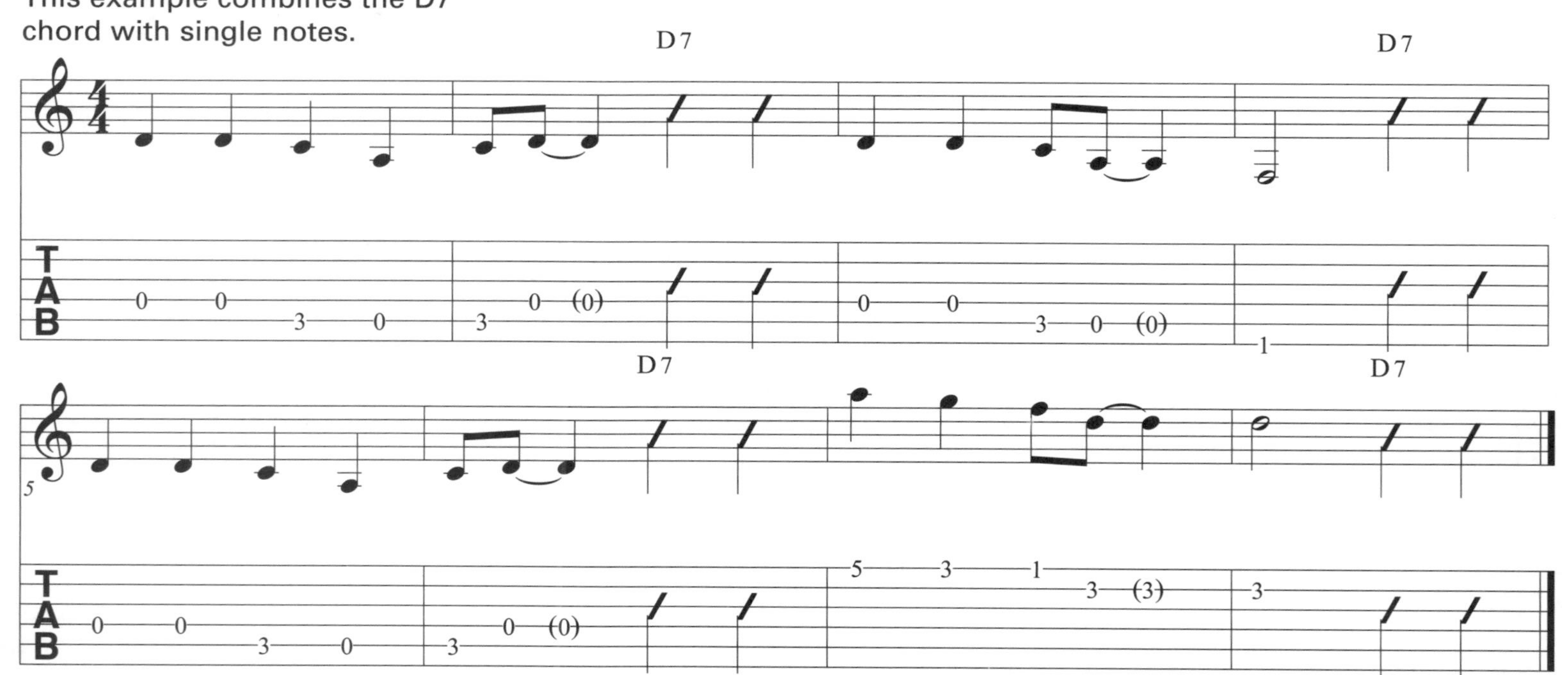